MEMORiES Cast Long Shadows

SO LIGHTEN UP NOW!

Bren Russell Campbell

Copyright © 2023 Bren Russell Campbell

Originally published privately in 2010 as 'Let it Go'
By Seahorse Design & Publications

In this format revised & updated 2022
This edition August 2023
Published by Amazon

All rights reserved

ISBN

No part of this book may be reproduced or used in any manner without the prior written permission of the copyright owner, except for the use of brief quotations in a book review.

I dedicate this book to Erika, my partner and best friend, who walked beside me on my darkest days, and shone a torch along the path until I could see my way again.

Special thanks to my dear 'Catkin' who has inspired me from the very start of my quest to take charge of my own body, and encouraged me to always believe in myself.

Illustrated with line drawings by Bee

CONTENTS

.... i
SECTION ONE 1
CHAPTER ONE 2
   am I who I think I am? 2
CHAPTER TWO 5
   the life of bren - why me? 5
CHAPTER THREE 11
   soul therapy 11
CHAPTER FOUR 14
   my body needed light 14
CHAPTER FIVE 17
   mind shadows 17
CHAPTER SIX 22
   standing in my own light 22
CHAPTER SEVEN 25
   moving on 25
SECTION TWO 27
CHAPTER EIGHT 29
   three steps to lightening up 29
STEP ONE - THE BODY 32
CHAPTER NINE 32
   eating lightly 32
CHAPTER TEN 43
   why detoxify? 43

CHAPTER ELEVEN	46
three of the best things in life are free	46
STEP TWO – THE MIND	49
CHAPTER TWELVE	49
lightening the mind	49
CHAPTER THIRTEEN	58
how stress causes dis-ease	58
the riverbank	60
CHAPTER FOURTEEN	61
mind how you think!	61
CHAPTER FIFTEEN	64
mind medicine	64
CHAPTER SIXTEEN	68
cell memories	68
CHAPTER SEVENTEEN	75
emotional freedom	75
STEP THREE – THE SOUL	80
CHAPTER EIGHTEEN	80
soul connections	80
CHAPTER NINETEEN	84
the seven heavenly colours	84
chakra healing	87
CHAPTER TWENTY	90
the magic of colour	90
CHAPTER TWENTY-ONE	94
soul assistants	94

SECTION THREE 101
   LIGHT-BRINGING 'SUPERFOODS' 102
      shopping for health 121
      SHOPPING LIST 122
   RECIPES FOR LIVING 131
      A Message from Bren 131
      Common food allergies include: 132
      EVERY DAY BREAKFASTS 133
      WEEKEND BREAKFASTS 136
      SUPER SALADS 138
      SALAD DRESSINGS 144
      COOL SUMMER SOUPS 149
      COMFORTING WINTER SOUPS 151
      LIGHT MEALS 156
      MAIN MEALS & SIDE DISHES 160
      SAVOURY SNACKS & TREATS! 168
      SWEET TREATS 173
   further reading 178
   FINAL WORDS FROM BREN 179
      remember to turn on your light! 179

There is no darkness so dense,
so menacing, or so difficult that it
cannot be overcome by light
Vern P. Stanfill

We can choose to see light,
or we can look on the dark side -
this book is about choosing the light
Bren Russell Campbell

SECTION ONE

THE BACK STORY

CHAPTER ONE
am I who I think I am?

I'm called Bren, which is short for Brenda. In Scotland and Ireland, it used to be quite popular, being of Old Norse origin. It means 'sword' or 'firebrand'. I was given that name at birth because my mother said she liked it, the reason being that she was a Viking from Shetland.

However, as a child I often wondered if it was because it had sounded cute when she introduced me and my twin brother when she walked us down to the village in our huge bouncy twin pram. 'Brian & Brenda, The Twins'.

And visiting the Shetland Isles as a teenager I became the source of great merriment for my brother, when he pointed out a smelly old boat called *'The Brenda'*!

I was born in November 1944, twenty minutes before my twin, in a remote Scottish farmhouse. A blizzard raged outside, and our father had to dig himself a pathway down to the village in knee-deep snow to fetch the doctor.

The family went to live in England not long after the war ended, and we moved around a bit until finally settling in Oxford – an amazing city to grow up in.

my light went out

As a child. I wasn't entirely clear about who I really was, but I did my very best to comply with what was expected of me, by my parents – especially my mum, my twin (although that was tricky because he was a boy and I found that boys could do as they pleased much more easily than girls), my friends, and my teachers.

I got into quite a few scrapes, but fortunately my dad always stood up for me and I would run to him for support if ever I was expecting a telling-off from my mother! This happened with repetitive regularity if I remember correctly.

Apparently, I was a bright little girl, and my memories of childhood are mostly very happy. However, I do remember a constant need to prove myself and wondering why my twin seemed to sail through life without having to justify himself at all. But as I say, he was the boy, and I was the girl.

I learned that compliance was the easiest way out of most situations. However, once I finished school and left the shelter of my family, things didn't always run smoothly.

Various traumas and personal challenges dogged me throughout my adult life, and these cast many dark shadows in my subconscious mind.

An exceptionally disturbing event, that caused untold damage, happened when I was a young art student in my twenties. The second of these major traumas occurred in my fifties. Twice, my world was turned upside down by events so awful that I was unable to deal with them. I just pushed them to the back of my mind.

clouds, rainbows, and sunshine

The second of these was the final straw. My sun seemed to set behind a cloud and never rise again. I saw myself as an unlucky victim, washed this way and that in the current of life's turmoil. I allowed darkness to invade my mind, my spirit, and eventually my body. I got cancer.

Finally, rainbows appeared beyond the clouds, helping me to move away from that dark place and allowing my sun to shine again. Putting the light back into my body, mind and spirit has taken a while and it hasn't always been easy, but I am still here, stronger than ever, so I reckon that must prove I got it right!

I know what I learned will help others in the same boat as me; it's a three-step method that I originally shared online for fifteen years and published little booklets that I gave away to anyone who needed support and advice. It's all in one book now; in it I explain why we need to deal with bad things when they happen, otherwise they leave dark shadows, and we carry this baggage around until it creates blockages in our body's energy system. I now believe that these are what eventually makes us ill.

After a roller-coaster journey of self-discovery, with help from many sources, I don't have any cancer now and I have learned a lot on my journey back to good health. Nobody really knows what makes a person ill, but one thing for certain is this: if our body, mind, and spirit are invaded by darkness like mine was. we cannot be healthy.

You can read the rest of my story by continuing to Chapter Two in this section. But if you want to find out about the programme that helped me to genuinely take control of my life, go straight to 'SECTION TWO'.

CHAPTER TWO
the life of bren - why me?

Everyone's life has its ups and downs, dramas, and traumas, that shape them into who they are, but the first five decades of my life read like an adventure novel! If I had been a cat, I would have used up my nine lives long ago!

Among many other tricky situations, I was rescued from drowning not once but twice, got knocked down by a car whilst crossing the road and climbed virtually unscathed out of my sturdy estate wagon, after it was crushed by a huge falling tree on my way home after doing the village school run. The car was a write-off, and sadly so was my marriage not long after that.

'What doesn't kill you makes you stronger!' I would declare casually. In fact, I had so many narrow escapes that people often said, 'Gosh, you're lucky to be alive!' But every time, after being subdued for a few days by these dramatic episodes, I just carried on. Although highly unpleasant, these were mere ups and downs compared to the major traumas of my life.

The first actually happened not long after I left home and returned to my birth land of Scotland, to study art and to make my way through life as an aspiring adult. It affected me so deeply that I couldn't bear to think about it, let alone discuss it with anyone who could have helped me to cope with my deeply buried feelings.

joy, heartbreak, and loss

Away from my mother's watchful eye, college life was more fun than I had ever dreamed of. I was a happy-go-lucky art student of twenty-two when I discovered I was pregnant. Back in the 1960s there was no support system for unmarried mothers like there is today and I was faced with a terrible choice. Hardly able to look after myself, let alone a child, and threatened with rejection by my family, I was forced to give up my new-born son for adoption and it broke my heart.

I returned to college, but I often skipped classes to visit a married friend who had given birth to her own little boy, round about the same time as me. She was delighted to let me play with him and take him for walks in his pram, while she went to a local café to meet her chums for coffee and a cigarette. When I brought him back, instead of returning to college, I would often go home and cry bitter tears, life seemed so very unfair.

I wasn't the only girl at the college to fall pregnant after the infamous 'summer of love' in 1967. Like me, another student was not able to keep her child and her little daughter was given up for adoption as well.

But two other students at the college kept their babies and from time to time they would bring them in to classes if their families couldn't look after them for the day. Everyone made a fuss of these tiny tots in their pretty wickerwork Moses baskets but I hid my tears and wondered how people could be so different; my mother refusing to even discuss my circumstances while these two unmarried mums had families who rallied round and happily welcomed those new little people into their lives.

Instead of throwing me out for lack of attendance, my understanding tutors allowed me to re-sit my third year, and I eventually graduated from the art college and trained to be a teacher – just like my mum. At least I could do something to make her proud.

However, my heart wasn't in teaching, and three years later, after marrying my boyfriend, we were blessed with a second son, Gregor. But he was only a few months old when a 'positive' smear test meant that I had to undergo a total hysterectomy. At only twenty-seven years old, the shocking truth hit me – no more babies for Bren.

This boy became my reason for living, and it was a joy to see him grow strong and tall, along with his twin brothers, who joined our family when they were three years old. I had hoped and prayed that my first little boy would be given a better life than I could possibly have managed and when our local paper advertised a big drive for fostering and adoption I never hesitated to apply. I would give these two wee boys all the care and love that I could never have given my first child. In my head I believed I was paying off karmic debt.

Gregor was delighted to have two little brothers to play with and our children grew up as free spirits. We lived in a remote croft on a beautiful Scottish island, and they thrived in the clean fresh air, digging ditches and playing commandos in the nearby forest.

After the many ups and downs of teenage life they all decided upon different careers. But, perhaps wary of becoming a pushy mother like my own mum, I always I let them make their own decisions, whether I agreed with them or not.

The twins, who both hated school, left the minute they turned sixteen and got work wherever they could find it, in hotels and garages. Gregor, having at first planned to study at art college, decided that he would rather find a job and start earning money too. One of the best paid jobs around was on the clam boats, so after six-months exploring South Africa and Zimbabwe with his girlfriend, he came home to the island and found work at sea.

But one dreadful night in May my world collapsed for a second time when I got a phone call to say that Gregor was missing from the boat. After a three-day search I was told that his body was found 'within water'. He had fallen from the deck and had suffered a fatal heart attack when he hit the icy water. He was only twenty-four and my life was overshadowed by devastating darkness.

I had never felt such hopelessness. Not only had my first child been taken from me, but now my second son was gone from my life forever. My remaining two sons, whilst themselves struggling to cope with the loss of their older brother, suffered even more when I, their mum, seemed to have lost the will to live.

Life became meaningless as I strove to accept the unfairness of it all. My doctor sent me for bereavement counselling, but memories were often too hard to bear. Instead, I consoled myself with drink and drugs that did little to help my depression. Every day I asked myself in despair 'why me?'

turning point

After years of suppressing my true feelings, I had reached the year 2001 when the doctor told me I had breast cancer. I felt numb. From a distance I heard my own voice agreeing to surgery, chemo, and radiotherapy.

However, after two sessions of chemotherapy I returned for a third, but shortly after having the needle inserted, I felt an agonising pain in my hand. The vein had collapsed, and I felt the pink poison burning my flesh.

I was sent home to recover, and asked to return the following week, but that night I heard a powerful voice in my head crying out, 'Your body says NO to this treatment', and at that moment I resolved to look for an alternative path towards my healing.

Having no idea where to start back then, but knowing where I did not want to go, I began to search the internet and uncovered many cases where people had recovered from cancer, usually described as 'spontaneous'. I told myself, 'If they can recover, why not me?'

Reckless and foolhardy was what some of my friends thought, but I closed my ears. I was on a mission!

Years later, with the wisdom of hindsight, I realised the key word should have been intuitive rather than alternative, because I did return more than once for surgery and did eventually agree to radiotherapy.

But the path I took was right for me, a combination of science and spirit, and I truly believe I am here today because I persevered and found 'my way'.

but where would I start?

In the course of my wanderings around the internet, I came across an Angel Healing Forum and through chatting online to a charming, gay Irish man called David, I was put in touch with a lady called Nina who described herself as a 'Soul Therapist'.

Magically she lived not far away from me and, even better, she was able to see me that same week.

At that point in my life, I was feeling very lost and lonely, but I very soon learned that we are never alone. Meeting Nina took me on the first tentative steps to becoming healthy again by nourishing my soul.

CHAPTER THREE
soul therapy

I had never heard of a soul therapist before I met Nina. When she welcomed me into her beautiful home in the Scottish borders, I was immediately aware that it was filled with the most wonderful energy. She herself seemed to glow and I later realised that it was her 'aura' shining with the radiant light of the Universe.

I was shown into a quiet room filled with fragrant scents and heavenly music. All around were lovely pictures and angel ornaments of every shape and size. Nina laid a beautiful crystal, the size of a duck egg, over where she told me my 'heart chakra' was and sat beside me with closed eyes, holding my hand. I felt myself relax completely and drifted off to sleep.

When I awoke, she handed me a glass of pure water and whilst I sipped it, she told me that she had seen me surrounded by healing angels who would help me on my journey of recovery. Her own 'guide' had come forward and asked her to tell me that, to move on, I needed to change my diet.

Nina assured me I was to trust that teachers would appear whenever I was ready to take the next steps. She used a word I had never heard before – serendipity.

On the drive back home to Edinburgh, with my partner and best friend Erika, although I was still wrapped in a warm glow from my experience, I was also puzzled by Nina's message. Why was I being advised to change my diet? We didn't live on junk food and neither of us was overweight. It hadn't been at all what I was expecting and, to be honest, I couldn't see the connection at all.

But a few days later a book arrived for me called *'Your Life in Your Hands'* by a Professor Jane Plant. Erika had gone online and searched *'links between breast cancer and diet'*.

This book drew very clear connections between dairy produce and hormone-based cancers, so she ordered it. Apparently, the author was a research chemist who had studied the incidences of breast cancer throughout the world. She proved without doubt that breast cancer and commercially produced dairy and meat products are linked. Breast cancer feeds on the high levels of hormones in intensively reared dairy cows.

So, I did need to change my diet – but I hadn't a clue how to start going about doing it.

the path unfolds – serendipity

A couple of weeks after that, Erika picked up a young woman in her taxicab, from a cash and carry supermarket. Box after box of lentils, mung beans, tofu and fresh vegetables were loaded into the boot. 'Don't tell me', said Erika to her passenger, 'You run a vegetarian restaurant?'

This was exactly right, and Erika promised to bring me there for a meal, telling the woman that we had gone vegan for the benefit of my health. From her bag the passenger gave Erika an invitation card to a lecture in Glasgow the following Sunday, *'Introduction to Natural Nutrition by Barbara Wren'*.

It was something I would never have thought of doing, but now I was beginning to understand the meaning of 'serendipity'.

Curious, I went through to Glasgow and from the very first sentences that this remarkable woman spoke, I was hooked, and I embarked on step two of my quest for health.

CHAPTER FOUR
my body needed light

Taking my seat in a lecture room at Glasgow's Caledonian University, I wondered if this would turn out to be the right thing for me to do.

Barbara began by declaring that our bodies always strive towards perfect health, but that often we don't heed what they are telling us. She explained that we must listen to our bodies because illness or dis-ease is the body's way of telling us that all is not right. It is sending us signals that we need to adjust certain aspects of our lifestyle.

a wake up for Bren

I was reasonably interested in finding out more about the course when Barbara said something that made me sit up and listen intently! *'Cancer'*, she said, *'need not be a death sentence; instead, we can see it as a wake-up call from the Universe.'*

Wow! This was more like it, so for the rest of the talk I was enthralled and signed up afterwards to study for a Diploma in Natural Nutrition.

And so began my next lesson – learning the secrets of introducing light to my body.

our inner power

On the first stage of my journey Nina had shown me how to welcome the light of the Universe into my soul. She had said that I needed to change my diet and promised that the right teachers would appear when I was ready. Now I had found my next teacher – and my healing journey continued!

I learned that we all have the power to heal from within, everything in the Universe is connected and we can harness the natural healing cycles that exist within us all. Finding out that our bodies require light to survive was so obvious – when I started to think about it!

I made a new friend at the college, Cathie, who became an inspiration to me on my healing journey. She had rid her own body of a non-Hodgkin's lymphoma, by putting herself on a diet containing so much carrot juice that she appeared quite orange at times! She still one of my best friends today.

the missing link

I absorbed so much information from this course and the self-empowerment I gained was a revelation, but then one of our fellow students died of cancer. It shocked the whole class because she had the healthiest diet among all of us. I had become friends with her, and we travelled together to the college in her car.

She confided in me that she was going through a very nasty marriage break-up. Every journey was dominated by angry descriptions of the arguments she was having nightly with her husband, and his lack of concern about the cancer she was fighting. But she went to church every Sunday and one day told me she knew it was 'Gods Will' that she would die. Sadly, not long after, she did.

After her funeral, I struggled to think why this friend, with her healthy diet and deeply religious beliefs, had not been able to overthrow the cancer, and it was a 'light bulb moment' when I spotted the missing link. The dark and toxic emotions, which I knew she was harbouring must have finally overwhelmed her. She just hadn't been able to lighten her mind enough to rid her body of darkness.

Barbara had told us that when we are ill our bodies talk to us. But evidently, I wasn't hearing the message because the tiny lump in my breast kept coming back. I urgently needed to find the key: the darkness in my own mind needed to be identified and dispersed, or else I would go down the same path as my now deceased friend, and there was no way I was ready to do that – I still had too many things to do yet. But my MIND was a mess.

I had learned how to fill my SOUL with the energy and light of the Universe and qualified as a Reiki Practitioner. I studied Quantum Touch and Angel Therapy, replacing the despair I had felt for years with new hope and self-confidence.

I had learned the art of putting light into my BODY and achieved a Diploma in Natural Nutrition. Working in this completely unfamiliar territory had opened up a new way of living. But now I needed more help although had no idea where to find it. I was starting to wonder if this 'serendipity' was actually working any more.

However, just as Nina had promised, the magic key was handed to me in a most unexpected way. The most important and complicated part of my journey was about to begin, and my new teacher appeared, in the shape of a kind and patient man called Alan.

CHAPTER FIVE
mind shadows

Between my body and my spirit lay the uncharted and intangible territories of my mind and my emotions. Getting that precious light into my mind was now critical. I desperately needed to learn how, because I felt sure this was the only thing left.

I was at a complete standstill in my journey towards perfect health when a visit from an old friend turned out to be the most remarkable coincidence yet.

My friend Maggi was on her way to a house near mine, for a counselling session with someone who practised a healing method that I had never come across until that moment. My friend had not heard about me having breast cancer and her sympathy turned to astonishment when I told her how often I had visited the Breast Unit.

finding the key

'Bren,' she said, *'you need EFT' - it will give you the key that you are looking for!'* She explained that EFT, or Emotional Freedom Technique, is a form of counselling intervention that uses various theories of alternative medicine including acupuncture, energy medicine, Neurolinguistic Programming (NLP), and TFT (Thought Field Therapy). She gave me a phone number and before long I found myself joining a group of men and women, all of whom were looking for answers to their own various health problems.

I learned that what went on in my mind really mattered – it mattered more than I could ever have dreamed.

dark clouds

Unbeknown to me all those dramas and traumatic events that I experienced during my life had left dark clouds in my energy system, shutting down my emotions, hiding the light from my soul and finally damaging the very cells of my body. I was about to learn how to disperse them.

Within the safe environment of the group, I gradually unravelled a pathway that would release these unhappy memories and lead to my eventual peace of mind.

Whilst going through bothersome situations and experiences in our memories, we would systematically tap various acupuncture points on our bodies until all the blockages were cleared. We tested the effect that each situation had on our emotions, on a scale of one to ten before starting the tapping procedure. Then again when we finished. Many times, it only took one round of tapping to be able to rerun the scenes in our mind's eye with no adverse effect at all. It was amazing.

One by one the traumas of my earlier life were brought to the surface and examined. I learned how to accept that they belonged to the past. I would never forget them, but they would no longer hold any power over me.

the cloak of guilt

The most difficult blockages for me to pinpoint were caused by the deeply buried perceptions that I had held about myself since childhood.

These patterns had etched themselves into my subconscious until I believed that I deserved to be ill. But I learned that they were misconceptions that could be identified, dealt with and then released.

I discovered that what I had thought to be a fairly normal relationship with my elderly mum and my twin brother was in fact very toxic. The truth was that my mother, a retired teacher, had an overbearing need to control others, and my brother's drink problem had got completely out of control. He was beyond help, although our mother's continual insistence that I (his twin) could and should help him had made me feel ever more guilty and resentful.

For several years my widowed mother, who lived in England, had been increasingly demanding on my time. Despite having a registered carer, in the form of my brother, she was constantly on the phone, asking me to come and see her. This I did on a regular basis until I became ill. But then the cloak of guilt fell even more heavily on my shoulders because it upset her so much that I could not make the journey so often.

I was shocked when I uncovered deep jealousy of my twin brother. He would usually remain incapable with drink in his room during my visits, but my mother explained his absence by saying that he was often 'tired' and seldom came downstairs before evening.

Her defence of his selfish behaviour made me cross, but working backwards through my life I knew that even from before we were born, I had resented his presence in MY mother's womb.

Of course, it made me sad as well as guilty to know that I was failing to prevent my twin from slowly killing himself with alcohol. But, through the process of EFT, I understood that he, like me, could have worked out his hang ups, but that he did not want to. I had to accept that it was something out with my control, one of my life's lessons learned.

hidden resentment

So, it was a complete surprise when next I recognised how much resentment I was also harbouring towards my mother. During the EFT process I observed that throughout my life I had believed that she had always favoured my brother who, it appeared to me, could do no wrong in her eyes. On the other hand, I had never felt good enough to earn our mum's special smile, no matter how hard I tried. All my twin had to do, I recollected, was merely to walk into the room!

More importantly, I had never recognised how deeply damaging my mother's utter rejection of her first-born grandson had been. The guilt and shame that I felt because of her attitude and her insistence that this disgrace was never to be spoken of to anyone had hurt me incredibly, but I bore the pain silently, truly believing that I had indeed committed a terrible sin.

However, she still refused to talk about it - that chapter, as far as she was concerned, was closed. So, harder than acknowledging and dismissing my sibling jealousy was recognising how much guilt and pain I felt she had forced upon me, almost forty years previously.

The EFT sessions helped me to truly go back for the first time and properly remember those dark and difficult days. In the uncritical and supportive environment of Alan's group, I recognised and wept for the lonely and scared young girl that I had been back then, and I forgave myself.

I accepted that my mum was of a different generation and that I could never change her way of seeing things. I also saw how much of her existed within me and understood that many of the things that annoyed me about our mother were, in fact, aspects of myself that I needed to come to terms with. Surprising to say the least!

It would have been funny, if it wasn't so sad, that even as a woman in late middle age I had still been trying to receive that coveted special smile by being her good little girl, even though I secretly harboured genuine hatred of the way she had treated the younger me.

After dealing with the hurtful effects of that episode I faced up to a much more recent event. Incredibly, when my second son died, I had subconsciously told myself that I was being punished for giving away my first son and therefore did not deserve to be a mother.

Not only was I feeling understandable sadness and grief for my loss, I was also beating myself up with unnecessary guilt as well.

That heavy burden of remorse that I had carried around without question was finally being lifted from my shoulders. Gradually I learned to recognise and free myself from the subconscious energy blockages which, in my opinion, had contributed hugely to my illness.

CHAPTER SIX
standing in my own light

I felt an enormous rush of relief when I realised that my childish perceptions of favouritism were actually misconceptions. They could safely be disregarded because I was now a grown woman! When I saw that all my mum had ever wanted was what she thought best for her children, I felt a lifetime of dark thoughts float away. Instead of bitter resentment against my brother I began to remember lots of fun times we had all had as a family and realised how lucky we were to have had a mother who cared so much about us.

As for the shame of bearing a child out of wedlock, I accepted that my mother came from a different era in time. Society as a whole had not been ready to accept unmarried mothers and there were no benefits available, no provision for support or care as there is today. At last, I saw my mother as she really was, a lonely, vulnerable, infirm old woman. And at last, I could genuinely give her my love.

As a result, Erika and I persuaded mum that, in her final years, it made much more sense for her to come and stay with us in Scotland during the winters, and it worked out surprisingly well!

Mum was a little reluctant to leave my brother, but he was greatly taken with the idea of having some respite and promised he would drive himself north in time for Christmas. So, this decided it for mum, and she happily climbed into our car with her bags and her little dog, really looking forward to her holiday.

For the first time I felt sympathy towards my brother who, after all, given up his peaceful caravan in the woods and put his own life on hold to live with our quite demanding mother. He'd been a highly gifted artist, graduating with honours from a top London art school, but he'd put that all aside to please her. Having mum to stay for an extended holiday allowed me to see what a responsibility he'd been given since the death of our lovely dad in the year 2000.

Although dad had always been my champion, often standing up for me against my mum's criticism, I realised that his relationship with Brian had been quite different. I began to remember dreadful arguments raging between my father and my brother.

Our hard-working outdoor-loving father often seemed to be disappointed with his artistic and creative son, telling him to 'man up' and stop fooling around with his life. I saw how my brother's self-confidence had been damaged, first with our dad always badgering him to 'pull his socks up', and secondly by our mum constantly defending his behaviour and latterly making many of his day-to-day decisions for him, in her usual organising manner.

No wonder my twin was delighted to wave her goodbye for a few months! No doubt he went straight indoors for a stiff drink, but that, I realised was his way of coping with life. Mum couldn't change him either so, like her, I would just have to learn to love and accept him the way he was.

Her insistence on phoning my brother pretty much every day, which annoyed me greatly to begin with, stopped being an irritation when I realised how needy she had become since the death of our dad. Brian had done his best and it was good that I was able to help him have some respite.

growing up at last

Having my mother to stay helped me to establish a great shift in my perception of who I really was because very soon mum and I got along better than we ever had. I learned how to stop pressing her buttons, and at the same time I found that many of the things that had annoyed me about her were actually not very important.

We finally became friends and, when we chatted, I learned things about her life that I had never known before, which gave me an insight into what had made her such a strong woman – and me the woman I had become.

But she still wouldn't speak about the baby I'd given birth to so I decided that, out of respect for my mother's feelings, I should wait until she was no longer with us and then I would do whatever it took to search for and find my lost son. I reasoned that, with her being in her late nineties, I could surely wait a few years longer.

However, I wanted to do something so I placed myself on the register of birth mothers, in case he might contact me in the meantime.

CHAPTER SEVEN
moving on

In 2010 my mother passed on to that great school in the sky, but before she died, I was able to talk to her as an adult and a much-loved friend. This only became possible once I had taken my place as another woman in her life instead of her 'desperately trying to please but never quite making it' little daughter.

I felt very blessed that, at the end of her life, I was able to tell her honestly how much she meant to me, and how grateful I was for the lessons she had taught me. She was in the final hours of her life when I leaned over her bed and kissed her, telling her that I loved her. She gave me her special smile at last and replied, 'I love you too.' I was happy that she passed away, at the age of ninety-eight, knowing that she and I were finally friends.

Sadly, my twin brother only survived our mother for a short while before his body succumbed to the ravages of alcohol. He'd had a major drink problem since he was in his thirties and I learned that this had been entirely his choice, and nobody could have prevented it, not even me, his twin.

My two chosen sons both joined the army. One of them left and emigrated to New Zealand where he used his Army training skills to drive trucks for a living, while the other is still a serving soldier in the British Army.

I am so proud of them both. They both married and I now have many beautiful grandchildren who bring joy and light to my life.

joyful reunion

After my mother passed away, I did indeed look for the baby boy who was taken from me in 1968. Needless to say, the day I got the phone call from the specialist family finder to say, 'We've found your son!' was a moment I shall treasure for the rest of my life.

As soon as I could, I met my handsome forty-six-year-old son and his beautiful wife for the first time. It was a joyful reunion; we bonded instantly and are a constant source of happiness to each other now. We know that our souls have always been connected, even though it took longer for our physical bodies to meet again.

The voyage I found myself on, after that failed chemotherapy session all those years before, was scary, turbulent, revealing, and exciting. It threw me into unknown waters and at times I feared that I would be tossed out and drowned.

Thankfully, with help from both science and the Universe, I reached a safe harbour, but I will never stop learning and I am grateful to that dis-ease called cancer – it changed me for the better. I was given the opportunity to take charge of my own life and thus to facilitate my own healing.

I truly believe that cancer is not the death sentence it is often feared to be. Instead, I learned to see it as a 'wake-up call' from the universe for me to change the aspects of my life that I believe had made me ill.

Finally, after years of self-doubt, guilt and hiding my true feelings I discovered who I am. I have learned to appreciate the Dance of Life and it is my hope that my programme of light will help you to dance too.

SECTION TWO

THE LIGHT PROGRAMME

A note from Bren:

The Light Programme is compiled entirely from my own experiences and opinions. It is intended to be complimentary to any method of healing the reader has chosen. I would never suggest that it should be an alternative to conventional treatment.

For almost twenty years I went on a personal voyage of discovery and what I learned changed me for ever.

Initially I shared everything I uncovered on my website, which I called *The Light Programme*, and published several little booklets which I gave to anybody who asked for one. But now I have put it all into this one book, so that everyone can benefit.

Some of the concepts outlined in this section are unconventional, even controversial, but I have included them because I truly believe they make sense.

None of the suggestions are dangerous to anyone's health, so if this programme is embraced with an open mind, the benefits will far outweigh any effort involved.

There can be no doubt that enlightening Mind, Body, and Spirit to create balance within our whole self will ALWAYS have a positive effect.

CHAPTER EIGHT
three steps to lightening up

One of the most exciting and astonishing things that I discovered is that our bodies can only function correctly if we feed every part of them with LIGHT. It is such a simple concept, but very often we remain unaware until something happens that makes us stop and look for answers.

In **STEP ONE** I explain how we can choose foods that put light inside our **bodies**, and why we should do this.

STEP TWO: Depression is very common, and it's not always easy to switch our **minds** to think positively just like that. But here you will find simple ways that really make sense.

STEP THREE: Our **soul** connects us to the Universe. It's nothing to do with religion and everything to do with finding our higher self.

By embracing the idea of filling every part of our being with light instead of dark we see each aspect of our life improve. Balance is achievable by everyone.

Sometimes it may seem easier to give up the whole idea and revert to dark foods, dark thoughts, and dark feelings, and that's OK!

But please try to make these moments as short as possible because it really IS worth the effort, for ourselves and for those around us.

I'm not saying that we can cure every disease this way, but I am saying that we owe it to ourselves to give it a really good go! And then who knows? One day you may wake up and say, 'I am SO GLAD that I read that book!'

why light matters

***LIGHT is LIFE** If you put a plant into a dark cupboard, it will wither and die. Light is a natural requirement for life. Without light there is no life. Light is a miracle that everyone needs in their life.*

- Light increases oxygen and blood flow
- Light speeds up wound healing
- Light helps reduce pain and relaxes our muscles
- Light finds just the right places in the body to heal
- Light activates vitamin D synthesis
- Light lowers blood pressure
- Light increases heart performance
- Light improves arteriosclerosis
- Light lowers cholesterol counts
- Light helps in weight loss
- Light is effective against psoriasis
- Light promotes the production of sex hormones
- Light activates an important skin hormone
- Light is a nutrient like vitamins and minerals

what makes us whole?

Did you know that the word HEALTH derives from an Old English word, 'hælth', which means wholeness, in body mind and spirit?

Human beings are not just bodies because we also have a mind which is the control centre of the body, and a soul, that intangible spark that makes us who we are. Lack of light in any of these areas will eventually make us ill.

Our **bodies** can be lifted from darkness to light by making sure that what we eat is good for us. Changing to a light filled diet becomes easier the longer we do it. We feel so much more alive that it soon becomes second nature to abandon our old eating habits.

We can lighten our **minds** by letting go of the dark and heavy burdens such as grudges and resentments that we all carry around, often without realising. But we reap what we sow, so we must learn to dispense with hatred and sow love instead!

I believe it is our spirit, or **soul**, the magical spark of life that we were born with which defines our very being. Our soul connects us with the Universe, and when we learn to do this, we flood our higher selves with light.

Are you ready now to start your own very easy three-step programme for light and life?

You are?

Let's go!

STEP ONE – THE BODY

CHAPTER NINE
eating lightly

Before studying Natural Nutrition, I hadn't really thought about the fact that meat and meat products come from dead animals. Or that the ingredients in pastry, bread, cakes and biscuits, which I thought of as 'treats', are all made from products that have not seen any sunshine for a very long time.

But doing a Diploma in Natural Nutrition taught me that the sun, and the sun-attuned electrons in fresh fruit and vegetables, bring us to a higher level of energy, and to a higher level of development as human beings.

When we bring light into the food we eat, light is transported into our body.

our bodies are a factory

Perhaps you don't realise that your body is a fantastic factory that manufactures miracles inside you, every second of your life?

Inside our body there are around 200 trillion individual cells, all communicating by tiny pulses of light. If our cells are denied this precious life energy, we become cold, sluggish, and acidic, a breeding ground for disease.

But to operate at maximum potential our bodies need the best possible nutrition for every one of the millions of tasks carried out by these constantly pulsating cells. In our body every cell has its own special role. Some work all day to despatch the nourishment that activates our body's various functions. But when we sleep the work passes over to the 'night shift', whose sole task it is to detox and eliminate waste.

The day shift cells can only work correctly if they receive enough light, whereas the workers on night shift do not know how to process food – that is not their job! So, if we eat too late at night all that nutrition gets stored as fat – many an overweight person is a midnight snacker, so next time you have the urge to have a snack before bed, remember the night shift cells, don't burden them with food, they can't use it!

So, my view of eating changed completely, from merely supplying the necessary fuel for the body, to becoming one of the main ways of introducing light into our cells. We were taught that food which has very recently been alive in the fresh air and sunlight can be called light-giving food, which automatically nourishes us with 'earth energy'. People thrive on a diet of fresh food.

As the main cook at home, I delighted in this new-found knowledge. Fresh fruit and vegetables became a big part of our daily diet, meaning that my shopping habits changed as well.

Later on you will find a handy list of foods to add to your shopping list, and how they are good for you.

'veggy' basics

All the nutrients we need can be easily obtained from a well-balanced vegetarian diet. In fact, research shows that a plant-based diet is far healthier than that of a typical meat-eater.

As a general rule, so long as we eat a variety of foods including **grains, fruit, vegetables, beans, pulses, nuts or seeds**, a small amount of **fat**, with or without the dairy products, we will be getting all the nutrients we need.

Nutrients in our food can be divided into five classes:

- Proteins
- Carbohydrates
- Fats (including oils)
- Vitamins
- Minerals

And every one of these essential food ingredients may be obtained from non-animal sources.

it's a fact!

There are around 400 million vegetarians, worldwide. About 8% of the World's population is vegetarian, including around a quarter of India's people whose faith forbids them to eat meat. Medical research has shown that on average, lifelong vegetarians visit the hospital 22 % less often than an average meat-eater.

A study conducted several years ago by Oxford University concluded that vegetarians were 40 per cent less likely to suffer from certain cancers. Vegetarians are also 50 per cent less likely to suffer from gall stones and less likely to suffer from diet-related diabetes.

we can eat rainbows!

Fresh vegetables and fruit are bright and full of energy – especially when they are raw or very lightly cooked

WHITE LIGHT contains all the colours of the spectrum, and an exciting project is to eat a rainbow of food each day! This is a great way to get light into our bodies!

The better our food looks, colour-wise, the better it tastes. The colours of fresh food are bright, and they invite us to enjoy them. Try it and see for yourself: next time you make a meal pay attention to which colour sits next to which and wait for your family or guests to say, 'That looks delicious.' Bring colours into your life and you invite better health to come along too!

some colourful food suggestions

- RED tomatoes, peppers, strawberries
- ORANGE carrots, apricots, turnips – and of course oranges!
- YELLOW bananas, lemons, sweetcorn
- GREEN peas, spinach, kiwi fruits, leeks, courgettes
- BLUE berries, grapes, plums
- PURPLE broccoli, beetroot, blackberries, red onion, red cabbage

You will see that there is no meat or fish in that list. Although eating meat is not necessarily bad for us, it is 'dead food' and contains none of the bright vibrant colour that fruit and vegetables have.

The other way to get light into our body is by adding 'good fats' (EFAs or Essential Fatty Acids) to our diet. Find out about them next.

oil on water = rainbow = white light

Have you noticed the rainbow effect when you look at a puddle with oil floating on it? We know that white light when split becomes a rainbow. When we eat 'good oils' we bring full spectrum light into our cells.

It was a big surprise to me when I learned that contrary to what I had been told, some fats are actually GOOD for us, and we need them to stay healthy. We must include them in our food because they carry light into our body. They are the Essential Fatty Acids, or EFAs.

Omega-9 is made by the body when we eat nuts and seeds, but two EFAs, omega-3 and omega-6 cannot be made by the body, so must be obtained from foods or from taking supplements. The best-known source of EFAs is Omega 3, from deep-sea fish like salmon or cod, but vegetarians can delight in the humble flax seed.

flax – the miracle seed

Flax (or linseed) seeds have been a part of the human diet for over 5000 years. Cherokee Indians believed that the flax seed was as sacred as the eagle feather. They said that this small, nutty brown seed captures energy from the sun – vital to the body's life processes, and scientists of today know that this is true!

We can buy whole or more easily absorbed ground flax seeds in health-food shops and supermarkets. They can be sprinkled over cereals and hot dishes or made into a nourishing tea (see the recipe section). Be sure to drink plenty of water – I mean LOTS of water, otherwise the seeds absorb too much moisture from the gut, resulting in constipation. The seeds can also be sprouted and used in salads and sandwiches.

good oil is good for our health

Miraculously Omega oils bring light to our cells as well as a host of other health benefits, from reducing depression to helping our brain function better.

Conditions found to improve with the addition of EFAs in the diet may surprise you:

- o   Heart disease
- o   Osteoporosis
- o   Alzheimer's
- o   Deafness
- o   Dementia,
- o   Psychiatric disorders
- o   Rheumatism
- o   Joint inflammation

What's not to like? One of nature's miracles can be added to everyone's diet today!

acid attack

Disease loves an acidic body to live in – but not an alkaline one

The significance of this is important for everyone's health, but to someone with cancer it may make the difference between life and death. Cancerous tissues are found to be acidic whereas healthy tissues are alkaline – this is a fact.

The typical western diet is hugely acidifying. The most popular soft drink (fizzy diet cola) actually has the opposite of the desired effect and dehydrates the body; dehydration creates acidity, and acidity creates disease.

empty calories

Although we see many overweight people every day, we may not realise that, surprisingly, many of them are suffering from malnutrition. Put simply, many people are not eating enough of the right kind of foods to give them the energy to burn off the calories they are eating!

White sugar, bread, biscuits, crisps and confectionery supply empty calories and supply virtually no nutritional value. 'Bad fats' in cheap meat products, and ready meals, are high in cholesterol, while many popular bakery products contain unhealthy 'trans-fats' to give them longer shelf life.

Apart from causing obesity, empty calories are weakening the immune system, acidifying the body and allowing diseases to develop.

what is the significance of pH?

Acidity and alkalinity in the body are measured by the pH (potential of Hydrogen) scale. An acid body is unhealthy.

The pH scale goes from 0 to 14, with 7 being neutral.

Below 7 is acidic and above 7 is alkaline. Water has a pH of 7.0 and is considered neither acid nor alkaline but neutral.

The blood, lymph and cerebral spinal fluid in a healthy human body are designed to be slightly alkaline at a pH reading of 7.4.

Cancer cells cannot survive in an oxygen rich environment. At a pH slightly above 7.4 cancer cells become dormant and at pH 8.5 cancer cells will die while healthy cells will live.

cancer and pH

In Holland, a Dr. Moerman spent forty years developing an alkalising nutritional programme which was accepted by the Dutch government as a legitimate treatment for cancer. Results indicated that Dr. Moerman's diet, which alkalised the body and boosted the immune system, could be more effective than standard cancer treatments.

Many of nature's natural foods are filled with disease fighting properties and can be an extremely useful tool in our battle against illness. Changing our eating habits can be a significant contributing factor in managing sickness.

Our food can make us acid or alkaline, but unless we are doing a detox there is no need to go mad! Eating 80% alkalising foods will do us a power of good.

But, if we are receiving treatment for cancer, doing our best to eliminate acid-forming foods altogether – see the lists below, will give our body the strength we need.

alkalising (eat 80%)

- Fresh fruit & vegetables
- Steamed or raw veg
- Millet, quinoa
- Wild & brown rice
- Sprouted grains and seeds
- Whole seeds
- Most fruit and berries
- Herb teas & green tea
- Kombucha & Kefir
- Free range eggs
- Organic cottage cheese
- Extra virgin olive oil
- Cod liver oil or Flax seeds

acidifying (eat 20%)

- Refined grains & flours
- White bread, pasta & cereals
- White sugar
- White rice
- Sweeteners
- Alcohol
- Factory hens eggs
- Fizzy pop
- Coffee
- Meat & fish
- Dairy products
- Microwaved food
- Ready meals

there is good salt and bad salt

Common table salt (sodium chloride) has had all the minerals taken out of it and it dehydrates your cells which drives oxygen out of them. This makes your body too acidic. Cancer and heart disease love an acid body - so think twice before shaking it all over your food!

Instead of ordinary salt, look for natural crystal sea or pink Himalayan rock salt both of which contain the essential trace minerals like potassium, iron, and calcium that are taken out of table salt.

Notice that food packet labels often only declare the sodium content of salt (Na) instead of the true level of salt which is Sodium Chloride (NaCl).

salt and cancer

Salt (sodium or sodium chloride) is used to flavour foods and as a preservative. Diets high in salt have been linked to an increased risk of stomach cancer. High blood pressure can also be caused by having too much salt in the diet.

The body does need some sodium but in most cases, we get all our sodium requirements from foods naturally. There is no need to add salt to foods. It is a good idea to switch to a low-salt diet and try flavouring foods with herbs and spices instead.

Often lots of salt is hidden in packaged and take-away foods so when shopping, read labels and choose products with less sodium. Look for 'no added salt' or 'low salt' foods, and be aware that many food labels only give you the sodium (Na) content which means that the true salt content (NaCl) is not declared.

sugar

Sugar in the diet is not a known risk factor for cancer by itself. However, eating too much sugar will affect our health negatively if it leads to weight gain, as being overweight or obese increases the risk of developing cancer of the bowel, kidney, pancreas, oesophagus and endometrium (uterus), as well as breast cancer in post-menopausal women.

Avoid eating too many high-sugar snacks like chocolate, lollies, biscuits, cakes, and soft drinks. Instead choose nutritious foods such as fruit, vegetables and wholegrain cereals and always drink plenty of water.

hormones and the dairy cow

We must remember that cow's milk is designed to turn a small calf into almost a ton of beef in under a year. It is full of fatty acids and, if not organic, the animals' diet is boosted with even more growth hormones. Most humans cannot properly digest the enzymes in milk beyond weaning, and it just get stored as fat.

There used to be strong links between lifestyle and diet from East to West – most notably that the traditional Chinese diet did not include dairy produce. Statistics published in the year 2000 showed that 1 in 10 women in the UK would develop breast cancer whereas the incidence in China was just 1 in 10,000.

But today American and British women have *a 1 in 7 chance* of getting breast cancer, a hormone-dependant disease. And sadly, as American fast food restaurants gain popularity in the East, occurrences of breast and prostate cancer are increasing too.

Studies now show that cancer is much lower in developing countries than it is in 'Westernised' countries. People in these countries eat a low fat, high fibre diet that consists mostly of vegetables, fruits, and whole grains. Cancer is very rare where the diet consists of fresh food.

If you really feel your family cannot live without dairy milk, I would urge you to consider buying organic. Although slightly more expensive organic dairy livestock can't be treated with antibiotics and are instead often treated with botanicals or vitamin supplements.

Organic milk has a longer shelf life than regular milk and is high in Omega-3 fatty acids, because it comes from drug-free, open pasture cows.

CHAPTER TEN
why detoxify?

From childhood onward we subject our bodies to substances which they are not designed to cope with. This is bad news for us all, especially our children.

Hormones, steroids, antibiotics, and pesticides are a few of the poisons appearing in our foods in the modern world of intensive farming. Organic foods might appear more costly, but what price can we put on our health?

City water supplies, using recycled water, can contain many different microscopic toxins that cannot be filtered out, from lead to deadly cryptosporidium, pesticides and poisonous algae, even hormones from millions of birth control pills and the dosing of animals to make them grow bigger and faster.

the fruit and water detox: 'lucky 13'!

That means 8 glasses of water plus at least 5 portions of fruit and vegetables every day.

Water is the most important nutrient for life! Without water, we will die in less than a week. With water, we get greater benefits from the nutrients we eat, better filtering of the toxins in our body (which must find their way out), fewer aches and pains, better sleeping patterns, fewer infections – the list is endless.

the magic of water

If you do only one thing for your health, drink a minimum of eight glasses of water daily. The benefits of water could fill a book – and the health costs of not drinking enough water would fill another.

Our bodies are made up of about 60% water and staying hydrated can affect us both physically and mentally.

Things like improved memory and mood, fewer headaches or migraines in some individuals, better weight maintenance and improved insulin resistance as well as improved exercise performance are all results of drinking enough water. Also, you'll suffer less from constipation and enjoy improved health of the urinary system.

Bottled water is expensive, although it certainly tastes better than tap water, but it is easy to install un under-sink water filter nowadays. However, a good quality filter jug makes an inexpensive alternative that everyone can afford.

Drinking eight glasses of water a day may seem like a lot, but if you have a glass of water when you wake up, one before you go to bed, a glass half an hour before every meal and three others through the day, you have achieved your target without hardly trying. The water helps flush away toxins and the good news is that you'll feel the benefits almost immediately.

On your 'lucky 13' regime you will find your appetite adjusts so that you don't need snacks between meals, and you'll find your desire for sweet things will diminish, naturally. Being properly hydrated not only improves your skin but can boost energy levels, improve mental alertness, and help avoid a host of ailments.

fruit & veg - nature's gift to our bodies

Eating at least five portions of fruit and/or vegetables daily will help boost your intake of antioxidant vitamins and 'phytochemicals'. They help to combat the damaging effects of toxins, strengthen your immune system and give you more energy.

how big is a portion?

- 1 small glass freshly squeezed fruit juice *or*
- 1 slice melon, pineapple *or*
- 1 apple, orange, peach, pear *or*
- 2 kiwis, plums, or apricots *or*
- 1 cup berries, grapes, or fruit salad *or*
- 1 Tbsp dried fruits eg raisins *or*
- 3 Tbsp cooked vegetables *or*
- 3 Tbsp grated raw carrot, cabbage, beetroot *or*
- 1 soup bowl heaped with salad leaves

This simple detoxifying regime will leave you feeling cleansed, energised and ready to face the days ahead with renewed enthusiasm and vitality. If you are ill, it will help you to recover your strength.

Whether we are ill or not, we can all benefit from this easy detox every now and then.

CHAPTER ELEVEN
three of the best things in life are free

I don't understand why children aren't taught in school that three of the most basic requirements for good health are absolutely free!

WATER – the free miracle liquid

- Water lubricates the joints
- It forms saliva and mucus
- It delivers oxygen throughout the body
- Water boosts skin health and beauty
- It cushions the brain and spinal cord
- It regulates body temperature
- The digestive system depends on it
- Water flushes out body waste

SUNSHINE – the free gift of light

- Sunlight can improve mood
- Sunshine may prevent us from over eating
- Sunlight helps stimulate the body's production of vital vitamin D
- Sunshine can help clear up skin conditions like psoriasis.
- Sunshine will strengthen your bones

FRESH AIR – doesn't cost a penny

- Fresh air is good for your digestive system.
- Fresh air improves blood pressure and heart rate.
- Fresh air makes you happier.
- Fresh air strengthens your immune system.
- Fresh air cleans your lungs.
- Fresh air gives you more energy
- Fresh air gives you a sharper mind.

Don't forget that Oxygen is essential to maintain an alkaline body, so plenty of fresh air is really important. Most people do not breathe deeply, so they lose the benefit of much of their lung capacity. Most indoor air is ten times more polluted than outdoor air, but most of us spend up to 90% of our time indoors. And need we mention the importance of non-smoking? You know it makes sense!

BONUS – this energy force is free too

One of the most encouraging aspects of my new lifestyle was that I began to believe that anything is possible, I just had to switch my energy from negative to positive!

It gradually became obvious to me that some kind of hidden force, or energy is at work everywhere, all the time. And although unseen, it is so powerful that it affects physical matter.

Look at those wonderful flocks of birds and shoals of fish, who move and turn together at the exact same moment. They clearly demonstrate this unseen energy for everyone to see if we only look.

People in the Far East have been aware of it for thousands of years – they call it 'chi', or 'Qi' - and believe it to be the natural energy of the Universe, which permeates everything. From healing their bodies to arranging their homes, offices, parks and playgrounds they constantly strive to recognise the chi and balance it perfectly.

I bought books on Feng shui, sometimes called Chinese geomancy, an ancient Chinese traditional practice which claims to use energy forces to harmonize individuals within their surrounding environment.

The term feng shui means, literally, "wind-water" (i.e., fluid). From ancient times, landscapes and bodies of water were thought to direct the flow of the universal Qi or Chi, "cosmic current" or energy –

I enrolled on a course to learn Reiki, a technique from Japan that realigns and balances the energy field around a human body. We practiced on each other, and I was surprised and pleased when other pupils reported positive results when I worked on them.

Learning Reiki gave me a surge of personal empowerment and responsibility, which has benefited me ever since. I now know that I alone am responsible for the way I feel and that it will affect my body.

I also know there is definitely an unseen, very powerful positive energy that we can connect with whenever we want, and that it is absolutely FREE!

STEP TWO – THE MIND

CHAPTER TWELVE
lightening the mind

Positive (LIGHT) thoughts give us energy & strength
Negative (DARK) thoughts rob us of power and health

LIGHT thoughts

- I FEEL POSITIVE
- I FEEL HAPPY
- I HAVE ENERGY
- LIFE flows through MY body
- I FEEL GOOD

DARK thoughts

- I FEEL NEGATIVE
- I FEEL GLOOMY
- I FEEL DEPRESSED
- I FEEL LAZY
- I FEEL ILL

thinking about thoughts

We can switch our thoughts if we want to!
We may not change events - but we can change how we react to them.

We are what we think we are!
Every thought we think creates our health and circumstances.

Thoughts are seeds that we plant in our mind
The more we hold onto a particular thought, the more power we give it and the stronger it will grow.

Thought for today
What am I worrying about today
that has really nothing to do with me?

Thought to remember
Yesterday is gone, tomorrow is a mystery, but today is a gift – that is why we call it the present.

what are YOU thinking right now?

Be aware that positive thoughts are light thoughts. Negative thoughts are dark.

We need to listen to our thoughts because it is often a big surprise to realise how much negative thinking that we do every day.

How often do you catch yourself being self-critical, unforgiving, impatient, cross, 'beating yourself up'?

When you feel anxious, upset, nervous or angry you must learn to 'lighten up' – it could save your life!

give yourself a good talking to!

How often do you praise yourself? Do you ever say, 'Well done me'? It's healthy to feel good about yourself. You should be your own best friend, not a constant critic.

Instead of always looking for faults in yourself and the world in general, you can start to recognise your thought patterns, and replace the negative with positive messages.

You cannot think cheerful thoughts and be dragged down by self- criticism and worry at the same time.

So, you have everything to gain by observing what goes on in your head and replacing the bad or sad thoughts with glad ones! Even making small changes to the way you look at life can have an astonishing impact on your health and well-being.

- o   Positive thinkers enjoy better health
- o   Positive thinkers have better relationships
- o   Positive thinkers have more confidence
- o   Positive thinkers are more successful in life
- o   Positive thinkers have a happier life

Even if you do not believe it will have any effect, start anyway – you have nothing to lose!

decluttering the mind

Sometimes we feel we have too many things on our mind.

After questioning over 3,000 people, a survey found that 72% of people said they were constantly worrying about money…and this was making them feel stressed out, taking their focus off other important areas of their lives.

Advice from a money expert is straightforward:

Take a close look at your spending habits and financial situation, make a budget, and stick to it. Set savings aside for emergencies and retirement and keep your financial records in order. Finally, consolidate debt and avoid unnecessary expenses. You might increase your income by finding new ways of making money or improving your skills. Whatever, stop worrying and do something.

so, how do we lighten our mental load?

We need to 'clean' up our thoughts. One technique is called the brain dump and we only need two things to do it - a pen and a piece of paper! What we're going to do is just write down whatever's on our mind for fifteen minutes or so.

Whatever it is, all the tasks, all the stuff, all the things that we're thinking about, whatever they are right now, just start writing. It's best to use paper and pen, not computer screen and keyboard. Just get it out of our brain and onto the paper. That's it!

We can destroy the piece of paper or hang on to it – it doesn't really matter because we will feel better whatever we do. We will think more clearly, and our mental load will feel lighter – and we've DONE SOMETHING!

the power of thought

Our minds don't function well when our body is tired, but the way we think can give us more, or less, energy. The mind-body connection is incredibly powerful. What goes on in our mind is entirely our choice – remember that we cannot change what HAS happened, but we can decide how we react to life. We can lighten our minds.

Going through life seeing only the bad and the negative will make us ill. But someone who is already unwell can make instant changes for the better by taking control of their mind and choosing only positive thoughts – trust me, it works!

stress less – live more

Every new thing I learned on my journey towards good health pointed to the same truth: the body actually obeys the mind. It is a massively controversial concept because it implies that we can make ourselves ill just by the way we think!

How can that be true? Why would anyone WANT to get cancer for example?

Obviously, nobody would wish an illness like cancer on themselves – at least, not knowingly. And therein lies a very important point.

might there be there a 'cancer personality'?

It was an eye-opener to find an article on that very subject by an American cancer specialist Dr Douglas Brodie MD, who reckons that there is a relationship between cancer and personality types, and he says it has existed for centuries. Going back in history to the second century AD, Galen, a Greek physician famous for his astute observations of patients and for his accurate descriptions of diseases, noted that women with breast cancer frequently had a tendency to be 'melancholic'.

Dr Brodie found that many of his patients had a long-standing tendency to suppress 'toxic emotions,' particularly anger, usually starting in childhood. Throughout their childhood, they have typically been taught 'not to be selfish,' and as adults they take this to heart as a major lifetime objective, often putting others before themselves as a matter of course. They also tend to 'suffer in silence,' and bear their own burdens without complaint, as well as the burdens of others.

Of course, there is one very harmful outcome of bottling up all this toxic emotion – stress.

How one reacts to stress appears to be a major factor in the development of cancer, says Dr Brodie. He said that almost all of his cancer patients had experienced a highly stressful event usually around two years prior to the onset of detectable disease. This might be the loss of a loved one, loss of a business, job, home, or some other major disaster. That made sense to me, because four years before my cancer diagnosis my life had been turned upside down when my son died in that accident.

If you do have cancer, you must ditch the stress.

cut the cords that tie you down

If you fall ill, it is critical to detach yourself from situations where you are vulnerable to other people's negative influence. It is time to make yourself your Number One priority and cut those strings that are holding you down.

THIS IS NOT BEING SELFISH.

It is essential to get that 'feeling good' element back into your life because this is how the body manufactures serotonin, and as I have already said, when your body is being fed with this, your health improves in leaps and bounds. You need to praise yourself more and criticise yourself less, spend more time with those who cheer you up, and less time with people who bring you down.

There is every likelihood that stress is a major factor in the development of cancer, but many cancer sufferers unwittingly put extra strain on themselves by the way they handle life.

Do you ever stop to 'smell the roses' or is your life a constant race to get things done? Do you ever allow yourself to truly enjoy what you are doing without feeling guilty? Or do you always feel frazzled and anxious?

What happens to us when we're under a lot of stress? Our heart races, our breathing gets faster, our blood circulation and metabolism speed up. Our muscles tense, getting us ready to fight or flee. But we don't do either.

And the stress builds up.

check this out

American cancer specialist, Dr Brodie reckoned there are certain tendencies common to cancer patients the world over. I found his list extremely useful in coming to grips with my own mind and therefore my illness.

- Are you highly conscientious, dutiful, responsible, caring, hard-working, and usually of above average intelligence?
- Do you exhibit a strong tendency toward carrying other people's burdens and often take on extra obligations?
- Do you often 'worry for others'?
- Do you have a deep-seated need to make others happy, tending to be a 'people pleaser', with a need for approval?
- Did you lack closeness with one or both parents, resulting in lack of closeness with spouse or others who would normally be close?
- Do you harbour long-suppressed toxic emotions, such as anger, resentment and/or hostility that may have arisen in childhood? (Think hard here - you may even be unaware of their presence.)
- Do you react badly to stress, often becoming unable to cope with it?
- Have you recently experienced an especially damaging event (such as a bereavement) before the onset of detectable cancer?

If you do recognise any of these traits, it is time to stop, now, and look at the areas of your life that might be different. Remember we can only do this for ourselves, our life is ours to change if we wish.

brain picking

Discovering Dr Brodie's theories on the 'cancer personality' was the trigger to finding out about my inner self. I knew that my surgeon would happily remove bits of my body until there was no more me left, but I wanted to get to the WHY of my illness.

Now this was a serious challenge - I would have to work through all the old conditioning and rid myself of all those automatic responses that I believed were part of the real me.

It was disturbing to find that I could identify with virtually all of the points Dr Brodie outlined, but the big question was HOW do I change myself. Surely my personality was the real me - wasn't it?

At that point I was faced with the hardest task of my life: I needed to change the very essence of me to lose what had been eating away at my health. I needed to look deep inside myself and perhaps alter my whole way of thinking. I had to pick my own brain like never before.

The way of life that had been mine was not working. But I believed that my way of doing things was correct, that others were wrong if they disagreed with me. At the same time, I desperately needed the approval of others, I even pretended that my emotional needs were unimportant because I was afraid that people may not like me. And I really wanted to be popular.

In short, I was a mess: something was causing my body to rebel and create the cancer in my breast – not once but several times. I had returned for surgery several times before it dawned on me that my body was telling me something, and I had better start to listen.

CHAPTER THIRTEEN
how stress causes dis-ease

When we are worried, we release hormones, ready for our 'fight or flight' response but if we don't do anything, they ferment and create acid in the body. Cancer sufferers are invariably more 'stressed'.

Stress makes us breath quicker. Long, slow breathing makes us alkaline while rapid breathing makes us acid. So, staying calm does us good in more ways than one, both mentally AND physically.

Over 80% of our worries are about things which are either not important, or that we have absolutely no control over. We must help ourselves before we can help others.

Letting go of stress is easier said than done, I know that first hand. But it's a big help if we disentangle ourselves from the problems of other people, however hard that may be. At the end of the day, we can only ever sort our own life out.

It may seem selfish to be always putting yourself before others but think about this; will the world stop if you stop trying to be all things to all people? Why don't you lead by example instead.

The best we can all do is to help others do the same, certainly not to fix their problems for them. Many people don't realise that their worries are their own responsibility and gladly thrust them on to others; this is never a permanent solution as it makes everyone feel bad.

here are some stress-busting ideas

- At work, delegate tasks to others: trust them to get it done
- Prioritise tasks: don't try to do everything 'right now'
- Recognise what you can do, and also what you cannot do
- Go for a walk if you feel stressed – exercise burns off the those 'fight or flight' hormones created by stress
- Learn to say 'NO' to things that you do not enjoy
- Do something totally different; new memories create serotonin
- Take deep breaths – send more life-giving oxygen round your body
- Have a good laugh as often as you can – more serotonin!
- You can't change the world, but you can change yourself
- Always try to get a good night's sleep in a quiet, dark room. Our body makes the powerful detoxifying hormone Melatonin only when it is completely dark, so a decent sleep gives the body a head-start on its healing journey.

The wee story on the next page is about letting go of things which can make us stressed.

We carry so much around with us that should be left on the riverbank of life. When we learn to unburden ourselves, we feel so much lighter for doing so. Allowing our thoughts to lighten up will give us a renewed enjoyment of life and all its aspects.

the riverbank

I have told this story many times to my friends over the years. It is one of my favourite parables.

Two Buddhist priests were walking beside a river when suddenly a scream shattered the tranquil atmosphere; these holy men belonged to such a strict order that they were not supposed even to look at a woman, and certainly forbidden to touch one.

The younger priest marched on, eyes straight ahead, ignoring the sound. But his companion looked round and saw a young woman struggling for life against the fast-flowing current. He threw himself into the water, waded out and rescued the girl, carrying her to safety.

At the evening meal the younger one approached the other saying 'Brother, I am still shocked at what you did earlier today: not only did you look at that woman, you even held her in your arms.'

His friend said, 'That is true my friend, but whereas I left her on the riverbank, it seems you are still carrying her!'

If we should catch ourselves looking on the dark side of life, all we need to do is to give our minds a nudge and say, 'Hey, LIGHTEN UP!'

CHAPTER FOURTEEN
mind how you think!

Can you believe that the cells in our body know what we are thinking – and they will do as they are told?

Like most people, I had heard of the Russian scientist Pavlov and his famous experiments with dogs: how first he programmed the animals by ringing a bell before immediately placing food in front of them. And how soon the very sound of the bell would make the dogs drool, even without the food. But I never realised what that proves: that the mind has the power to change the body!

The phrase 'mind over matter' is so familiar we use it without thinking – but I was thrilled when I learned what it actually means. One day I found a book called 'The Secret Life of Your Cells' by Robert Stone PhD. The back cover reads 'The cells of your body, even removed and observed at a distance, know what you are thinking!'

Excitingly, I had stumbled upon the proof I was looking for, that the body obeys the mind – and I really needed to learn how to make my own wayward body do what my mind wanted!

Stone's astonishing book describes the work of a scientist called Cleve Backster who did experiments involving live cells harvested from living humans. One woman was given a movie to watch and when she reacted to sudden acts of violence the oral cells that had been collected from her became agitated at exactly the same time, but they were in a laboratory half a mile away!

the mind does tell our cells how to behave

During my research, I learned the meanings of some very big words, one of which is 'psychoneuroimmunology'. Literally this term means: the mind (psycho-) controls the brain (neuro-), which in turn, controls the immune system (immunology).

Whatever we think is up to ourselves – but remember, thoughts can be good, bad or downright dangerous!

Pavlov proved that thought initiates a physical response in dogs – but it is no different for humans. Whether dark or light thoughts. our body responds accordingly, but most folk don't know that the MIND controls the BODY.

Here's how it works: if, like Pavlov's dog, you think of your favourite food, your mouth starts to water. Even though there is no food in sight, the thought produces a physical response.

Picture someone you love and you start to feel happy. You relax and a smile spreads unbidden across your face. Again, the thought produces a physical response.

Does that mean that we can literally think ourselves well or perhaps even ill? Yes. I believe it does!

Changing the direction of our mind from destructive to constructive can be done.

In the next chapter I'll talk about visualisation – the mind medicine that is totally FREE!

But in the meantime, on the next page is a little exercise to prove to yourself how easy it can be.

try this little experiment:

Close your eyes and picture being with someone you love very much.

It might be a child, your partner or perhaps your much-loved grandparent. It could even be a pet!

Keep your eyes shut and try really hard to recreate what this person looks like, even how they smell, and hold it in your mind's eye.

Imagine you are giving each other a warm cuddle.

Now move your attention to your own face - are you smiling? I bet you are!

Next think of the worst experience you have ever had.

Perhaps you were very frightened, such as almost drowning in deep water - or maybe it was a traumatic event like an accident.

Really concentrate on the horror of this episode and picture yourself going through it again.

Now switch your mind back to the present moment.

Is your mouth dry or are you perhaps tense and trembling? At any rate you are more likely to be frowning than smiling.

Simple though these processes are, they actually demonstrate what we have just been talking about - that the mind definitely influences the body.

CHAPTER FIFTEEN
mind medicine

Although there is plenty of misinformation out there, we can always be selective. So, when we come across something interesting, we can decide for ourselves whether it is true or false. I found this on the internet and decided it was worth believing!

'Positive Thinking May be an Important Key!

'SCIENTISTS say they have found that one of the body's 'good mood chemicals' forces some cancer cells to commit suicide. They say that when serotonin is placed in a test tube alongside tumour cells of Burkitt's lymphoma the cancer kills itself....

'Professor Gordon said: 'Serotonin is a natural chemical that regulates people's moods keeping them balanced.

'An exciting property of serotonin is that it can tell some cells to self- destruct. We have found serotonin can get inside the lymphoma cells and instruct them to commit suicide. The team are now working on a way of using the phenomenon in a form of treatment.'

Exciting though this article is, it may be some time before we see a treatment for cancer patients using Serotonin. However, the good news is that we can start straight away with our own personal programme to manufacture this magical ingredient for ourselves!

- o **So, let's get the serotonin working for us**
- o **How? By practising self-talk**!

visualisations & affirmations

We can programme our brains through powerful techniques called visualisation and affirmation, two highly effective methods of overcoming sickness. Looking for proof I was delighted to come across accounts of people who had overcome serious disease, such as cancer, without conventional treatment. In fact, their healing was very often due to positive thinking.

By a lucky coincidence (synchronicity again) I happened to be in London at the same time as a supreme master of the subject, Martin Brofman. He was giving a workshop, so I bought a ticket and found him to be one of the most inspiring and powerful people I have ever met.

Thirty years earlier Martin had been told that he had an inoperable tumour on his spine – the doctors said he had terminal cancer and gave him only a few months to live. But after just two months of intense positive visualisation and affirmations he went back to his doctor and no trace of disease could be found.

After personally meeting and chatting to Martin at the end of his workshop I promised myself that from that day forward I would learn to re-programme my consciousness just like he had done. I bought his book 'Anything Can Be Healed' and discovered how to switch off the negative thoughts and replace them with positive ones. Just as Nina's guides had promised all those months ago, teacher after teacher appeared in my life.

practical help

Impressed by meeting Martin and inspired to follow his example I explored the internet (again) to find visualisations to do. I was very taken with the name of renowned healer Betty Shine so I wrote to her along with an order for visualisation tapes. She personally wrote me a beautiful letter, filled with encouragement, along with her tapes, which were fantastically helpful and incredibly easy to follow.

There is one session called *'Mind Medicine'*, which she recorded especially for people with cancer. I listened to it so many times that I almost learned it by heart. On it she describes, in her wonderfully relaxing voice, how we can all build a healing room inside our heads, which we can go to for help with anything from a headache to cancer.

In my virtual space I created a lovely room with windows overlooking the sea. There was a soft comfy couch for me to relax, and around me were shelves holding different coloured bottles of pills and potions, each one providing a 'cure' for whatever I needed healing from. All I had to do was to imagine taking them, knowing they would work.

Betty Shine's tapes laid the foundations for healing the cells of my body, and the knowledge that I could help myself to health made my self-belief blossom like spring flowers.

Of course, I found plenty of naysayers out there as well, but I told myself, 'Brenda, why would you want to believe what THEY have to say? You want to be a success story, not a victim!'

the power of thought – affirmations

Although I was forced to accept that I hadn't been able to do without some medical intervention, I still passionately believed that I would get through this beastly cancer one way or another. Yes, that pesky little lump kept returning to the same place on my body – but at least it hadn't spread, so I was definitely getting something right.

I Googled the word 'Affirmations' and at the top of the list came the name Louise L. Hay. This remarkable lady, who lived to be over ninety years old, overcame a cancerous tumour as a young woman, without any conventional treatment. She has helped and inspired millions through her self-help books and her 'Affirmations' have been translated into many language.

I love her book *'You Can Heal Your Life'* because from start to finish it offered me the hope and encouragement that I so desperately needed. Her words on breast problems gave me much food for thought because I could completely identify with her definition:

'BREAST PROBLEMS: A refusal to nourish the self. Putting every- one else first....'

The corresponding mantra, which I wrote out and carried about with me reads, *'I am important. I count. I now care for and nourish myself with love and with joy. I allow others the freedom to be who they are. We are all safe and free.'*

CHAPTER SIXTEEN
cell memories

I had heard of 'cellular memory' but I wasn't sure what it meant. On looking it up I was not much wiser, but still very intrigued.

The idea, I read, is that people's cells hold memories of past lives and that those memories are activated by electrical impulses. There was no conclusive evidence that this is actually proven, but I was fascinated, nevertheless.

One day I was exploring the stands at an 'Angel Fair' in Edinburgh's Assembly Rooms, when I was drawn towards a clairvoyant sitting behind one of the tables. Instead of passing me a message from beyond the grave, which is what I had been expecting, the man said that he was compelled to tell me about a past life that I had experienced even though this had never happened before.

He told me that I had been a wise woman, a healer, in a previous life and that I still had the gift of helping others to heal. He knew nothing about me, but he added that I would be healed from whatever ailment was affecting me. He wouldn't accept any money, even though I offered, and his words left me feeling very enlightened. The thought that I might have lived before was utterly fascinating to me and I wondered a lot about it. But not long after that angel fair, serendipity handed me another gift that would satisfy my curiosity about this.

Even while I was studying nutrition, I still continued with Nina's Angel Therapy group meetings to nourish my soul, so when one day she offered us all a session of Past Life Regression, I immediately put my name down.

had I lived before?

It was to be a group session, for only a few of us, and would be divided into three sittings over a day.

In each sitting we would be guided back into a previous life and would learn something significant that still affected us today.

The idea that I was reliving events from three previous lives seemed much more significant than if they had merely been dreams. They resonated so deeply within me that I had to believe that they were based in truth.

I have recounted what happened in each of them below, not to sell the idea but to explain how they helped me.

Past life regression may well help others to uncover previously hidden fears and obsessions. Anything that opens the mind to allow light to flood in can only do good in my opinion.

After that day, hang-ups which had plagued me for years, guilt, neediness and a fear of being poor, slipped away, never to return. Many a time since I have caught the old mindset returning and sent it packing!

To me the concept of re-incarnation is very appealing, as it suggests that life does not end with death. When my son died, I wanted desperately to believe that we would meet again in the next life, and I studied book after book that would confirm my hopes that death is not the end.

Past life regression was not the slightly creepy experience I thought it might be, instead it gave me peace of mind. It may not be for everyone, but it certainly worked for me.

my three past life sessions

Workshop leader Nina, who was also a qualified hypnotherapist, made sure that we were comfortably seated and then led us through a gentle relaxing meditation until we reached a deep, almost trance-like state. The only sound was Nina's voice, which seemed to be coming from a long way away.

She invited us to picture a corridor with many doors along it, all different. Behind each door, she told us, was a different life that we had experienced. We should choose one, and when we were ready, open it and go through.

the survivor

After travelling for some way along the corridor, and passing through a heavy door, I immediately found myself on a grassy hillside, picking wild flowers in warm sunshine. Following Nina's gentle background promptings, I saw that I was bare-foot and dressed in a simple cloth garment tied at the waist. I was a young girl – perhaps twelve years old, maybe a little older.

From above I looked down into the valley where I could see my village, but there was much more smoke than usual gushing from the roofs of the primitive dwellings that comprised it. I started to run towards my home, but a sound stopped me, and I looked round to see a boy that I knew waving wildly. 'Don't go down there!' he cried, 'The invaders have burned the houses and killed our people. We must wait until dark.'

He signalled me to follow him, and we made our way further up the hill along with the flock of sheep that he minded. We crept back after dark, and as he had warned, we found our people lying dead among the smoking ruins. The boy set about dragging the bodies to the river and cast them in while I looked around for food.

The next day we hid again as voices could be heard approaching, but it was only a group of survivors from a neighbouring village that had also been plundered.

The scene shifted to a later time, and we had made new friends of the strangers and rebuilt some of the houses. The women taught me to cook and sew and I found that I was pregnant with the shepherd's child. When it was my time, the women helped to deliver a boy child and all in all I found motherhood a very happy experience.

However, the story had a very sad ending. One day I had left my child asleep indoors while I went up the hill to gather berries. A ghastly repetition of the previous attack began to replay, and I saw a band of men riding through our village setting fire to the dwellings. Cowering behind a bush I watched as they set my home alight before galloping off in a cloud of dust. I rushed back to find my worst fears realised – my child had been murdered, and all my friends and family were gone. I was alone and I felt the tears running down my cheeks. I opened my eyes then and waited for the rest of the group to do likewise.

Nina came round to us in turn and when I described my experience, she told me that, sad though it was, reliving this experience would hopefully mark an end to the guilt I had been living with for being a survivor after my son's fatal accident. She told me that guilt was a very common emotion after the death of a loved one. The message I had learned was 'It's OK to survive.'

the poor child

After a break we came back to our seats for the next session. This time I found myself once more barefoot and ragged, but on a cold, wet cobbled street. I was a pathetic, skinny child holding a tray of matches which passers-by bought for small, dirty brown coins. Hanging on my arm was a very old, blind man, hunched and crippled, with a stick in his other hand.

When my tray was empty, we made our way down a narrow filthy alleyway to a dark, smelly, and dingy room where the money was taken from us in exchange for a bowl of thin, tasteless but steaming hot soup. I fell asleep on a pile of rags before waking up and found myself back in Nina's lovely room.

When it was time to describe my experience, Nina suggested that I had reached my present life without releasing what she called 'poverty consciousness', but that it was now time to let it go. I realised that I had indeed always suffered from a fear of being penniless, even though I had never been poor. This had often deterred me from enjoying myself, through worrying about how much I was spending.

I was delighted to bring this subconscious hang up to the front of my mind and release it. From that day to this if I find myself asking 'can I afford that?' I immediately remind myself that the Universe will provide me with whatever I need! And never again have I felt the fear of being broke.

the peaceful end

In the previous two sessions one or two participants apparently experienced their own deaths although I had not. I reasoned that perhaps I was scared of the thought, so had avoided it. I wondered if I too would experience my death from a previous life.

In the final session after lunch I again found myself as a young girl but this time, I was well dressed in a stylish dark green velvet riding habit. I was standing in a forest glade beside my beautiful white pony and beside me was a handsome young man, also in riding gear, astride a fine horse. I was flirting and laughing, and I knew I was completely smitten by him!

But when I got back to my beautiful home I was sent to my room and could hear voices below talking about me. I knew there would be trouble in store for me, because I had been forbidden to see this man.

In the next scene I was being taken by carriage to a nunnery. After the great doors closed behind me, I was stripped of my fine clothes and given a plain, coarsely woven gown to put on. Being sent there had clearly been a punishment for defying my elders and I knew I would live the rest of my life behind those doors.

However, I found peace and happiness with my lot because other girls were brought to the convent, and I was always the one to help them. I became a wise and respected counsellor in that place and as I grew old, I gained the love and respect of everyone in the convent. In my old age I eventually became the Lady Abbess.

At the end of that life, as I lay on my death bed, I was surrounded by people who loved me, and I slipped away into my next life a content and peaceful person.

My fear of death gently floated away during this experience, and I now look forward it as a time when I will be reunited with all my loved ones who have gone before me, especially my darling Gregor.

I could say that attending that past-life workshop has helped to restore my faith, but to be honest I never really had much faith before the death of my son.

For a long time after his fatal accident, I almost lost the will to live because of the intense sorrow and sense of abandonment that I felt. The light really did go out of my life, and everything seemed grey and meaningless.

But now I know that this life, though precious, is not the end of the road. Nobody could call me religious, but I have gained an understanding of spirituality that has injected a new energy into me, and I don't think I would enjoy being alive half as much if I didn't believe that I will move on to another life after this one.

I say to those who scoff at such an idea that they will get a lovely surprise when it comes for their time to pass.

CHAPTER SEVENTEEN
emotional freedom

'The cause of all negative emotions is a disruption in the body's energy system.' So says Gary Craig, Founder of EFT. Gary maintains that emotional health is absolutely essential to our physical health and healing — no matter how devoted we are to proper diet and lifestyle, we will not achieve our body's ideal healing and preventative powers if emotional barriers stand in our way. This concept changed my life.

Every time someone else writes something critical on the wall of our mind it creates a negative blockage in our emotional body. Before we know it, we are carrying burdens that drag our spirits down and steal the joy from our lives. We find ourselves trudging along, becoming more and more bogged down until eventually, we get ill.

EFT opened my mind and gave me the missing key that allowed me to unlock the trapped emotions which I believe made me ill. I learned that our instructions for living are written on the walls of our minds and even as adults we subconsciously obey those rules. They are attitudes, opinions, and beliefs that we have accumulated over the years, hand-me-downs from parents, grandparents, teachers, religion, peers, books, TV and other so - called authorities in our lives. We are in effect robots, controlled by outside forces.

personal peace = perfect health

Discovering EFT was the major turning point in my journey. One of its key aspects is known as the Personal Peace Procedure.

This process is recommended for long-term work on deep seated health issues both physical and mental. For maximum success, we were invited to write down a list of every specific event in our lives that we wished hadn't happened, and then perform the EFT tapping routine on them one at a time. I guessed that I would find plenty!

baggage not needed on this journey

I couldn't believe how long my list became – what promised at first to be a very easy task turned into pages and pages of bothersome events. All those dramatic events from my earlier life had left their mark but some of them had been buried very deeply in my sub-conscious – although the scars were still there.

As I tapped away it was like un-peeling layers of an onion. It took quite a while, but as I went through my list, I could feel long standing hurts and grudges sliding away, never to return – emotional freedom indeed.

A happy effect of EFT is that we learn how to release countless other burdens and emotional baggage that we have been carrying around most of our life.

We all can learn how to change our mind for the better, by accepting that
nobody else has a right to put ideas into OUR head. It is up to us and nobody else to influence our state of mind and consequently our health.

letting it all go

On the journey I was on to find myself I learned some surprising, shocking, and often alarming things about the baggage I had been carrying around all my life.

During the early EFT workshops, we were encouraged to identify situations where we got angry or upset and I could think of hundreds. And a huge number of times it was an issue of me not being in control! I was a true control freak, but I didn't see myself as one. It was a breakthrough for me the day I saw that trying to control people or situations had merely caused me anxiety, bitterness and frustration, because the only person I can control is myself.

Ignoring my own needs, I had wasted a huge amount of energy trying to change other peoples' minds, their lifestyles and even their beliefs, but it had got me absolutely nowhere and only left me feeling useless.

In fact, putting myself into losing situations made me feel like a victim and, in my opinion, eventually made me ill. Believing that nobody understood me had made me feel angry, frustrated, resentful, worthless – the list of negative emotions had grown and grown, just like the lumps in my breast. I learned to stop looking for power in all the wrong places, pushing my point of view on to folk who were not interested and were so set in their ways that they would probably never change. Trying to organise the lives of others meant I was putting off thinking about my own affairs. I hid my neediness by making myself look useful and feel helpful.

I had to learn to let go and just be me.

All my life I had hated when people tried to control me, however, when my best friend pointed out that I myself could be bossy and domineering, I was shocked and a bit hurt. Admittedly I got stressed when people didn't do what I had visualised but surely that didn't mean I was trying to control them – did it?

You see the trouble was that I firmly believed I was helping my friends and family by showing them 'the right way' to do things - MY way! I wasted so much energy trying to change other peoples' minds, their lifestyles and even their beliefs but it got me nowhere. In fact, most of the time I felt that nobody understood what I was saying to them, and this made me feel cross, frustrated, resentful, worthless – the list of negative emotions had grown and grown, just like the lumps in my breast. I was looking for power in all the wrong ways, pushing my point of view on to folk who were not interested and were so set in their ways that they would probably never change.

Recognising and eliminating this toxic tendency was one of my most important discoveries. It involved serious introspection and questioning of my lifelong values; so it was far from easy, but I knew that somehow, I had to get rid of all this negativity or it would dispose of me.

BAGGAGE NOT NEEDED ON THE REST OF THIS JOURNEY

are you a control freak?

Here is a light-hearted quiz that I found in a women's magazine.

- You think you know what's best for others (your way)
- You make lists for everything in your life.
- You would rather drive than be driven
- As much as possible, you need to do everything yourself
- Other people's messes really bother you
- You rarely think that you're wrong
- You don't like people touching your things
- You like to know where your partner is at all times
- You tend to interrupt people a lot
- You don't like taking risks
- It's difficult for you to trust anyone
- You don't take it lightly when people disagree with you

Of course, I found that I could tick nearly every one of those boxes and facing up to the fact that I was a serious control freak was not easy!

But oh, what a feeling of relief when I accepted that the world would carry on perfectly well around me and I didn't have to do a thing! So, if you answered 'yes' to even a few of these questions it is time to stand back and just BE!

STEP THREE – THE SOUL

CHAPTER EIGHTEEN
soul connections

How do we connect to the celestial energy of the universe? It's not so difficult as we might think. In fact, the Universe is all around us and even just thinking about connecting with it activates our higher self.

Everyone knows that we all have a body – the physical part of us, and a mind – the bit of us that lives inside our brain and orchestrates our waking thoughts and actions. But we never stop to wonder what drives our mind.

It is our spirit, or soul, that magical spark of life that we were born with which defines our very being. Our spirit can connect our bodies and minds to a higher energy, freeing us from earthly worries and lightening our entire being. There are lots of ways to feel uplifted and most of them are absolutely free!

Joy and pleasure are two different things. Pleasure must be pursued again and again to be experienced. It comes from desire and disappointment and discontent take over when that desire is not met. But joy bubbles up from the centre of our being. When we feel joy, we are connecting with our higher self and our feelings of contentment last long after the experience.

music

Whoever described Music as 'love drawn from a higher plane and distilled for human ears' was spot on! We should all make time in our lives to listen to the kind of music which makes our hearts sing, no matter whether it be Mozart, or Guns and Roses.

Anyone who has sung in a choir or been inspired by a concert of wonderfully uplifting music knows that we are transported into a different, higher level of joy that can last for hours, even days after the event is over.

gratitude

Something I learned from the many workshops I attended on personal and spiritual development, was the miraculous effect that practising gratitude has on our well-being.

The first time I attended an 'Angel Meeting' we were all asked to sit quietly for a moment and count our blessings. I could see several folk in the room looking as if there was nothing much to be grateful for in their lives. But the group leader Graham, a gentle soul whose long hair, beard and loose linen smock made him look straight out of the Bible, explained that we can always find things to be grateful for. The very fact that we were able to come to this meeting and sit amongst like-minded souls for an hour or two made us very blessed.

He told us that if we can read, we are luckier than a billion people worldwide, who can't read at all. Over 75% of the world's population have no money, no bed of their own to sleep in and no prospect of a decent meal that day. After that we all wrote busily in our notebooks, thinking of all the blessings that we could count.

ways of freeing our spirit

Creative Expression of any sort is a really good way to nourish the soul. Drawing, writing, painting, cooking, indeed being creative in any way lets our intuition influence and guide our physical hand, prompting an upwards shift in our consciousness.

Laughing is such a good soul exercise! When we laugh, all the tension we feel dissipates. There is actually a bodily change, it helps our blood vessels to function better. It is important to laugh at something every day, even if it is only at ourselves.

Blessed are we who can laugh at ourselves, for we shall never cease to be amused!

Meditation, mindfulness and prayer are powerful methods of shutting out the busy turmoil of the world around us and achieving inner calm. When we practice these, we become humans 'being' instead of humans 'doing.' Research shows that people who meditate reduce their stress level and have a lower incidence of cancer.

When I was ill, I added myself to a worldwide prayer group where thousands of people prayed for those who had requested it, and I am sure that all that good energy helped me to get stronger.

Connecting with Nature is feeding our soul. So, we should walk among trees listening to the wind in the leaves and the song of the birds. In Bavaria it's an accepted method of finding inner peace and they call it 'Forest Bathing'. In Japan it is called 'Shinrin-Yoku', and it is a recognised therapy.

Researchers are discovering more and more astonishing facts about trees and the impact they have on people. Plants emit chemical substances that act like a natural antibiotic to repel pests, but these plant-based fragrances also have an effect on humans: even a short walk in the woods is enough to reduce the level of the stress hormone cortisol, while the body shows an increase in the production of the mood hormones serotonin and dopamine. Even several days after a forest bath, these and other positive effects are still in evidence.

Crystals hold the ageless energy of the universe within them. Crystals contain the remarkable ability to transform, absorb, amplify, and transmit. Energy is everywhere and crystals are the perfect conduit. In fact, the vibrations of crystals are known to change depending on the energy surrounding them, so every stone has a unique and different effect on each individual. Wearing or carrying a crystal or gemstone is a good way to absorb this ancient healing energy.

Children need no prompting to delight in the magic of being the first ever person to leave footprints in freshly fallen snow – why should we adults lose out?

When we connect with the Universe, we discover there's a big difference between the experience of joy and what we perceive as pleasure.

CHAPTER NINETEEN
the seven heavenly colours

The spectrum has seven colours which make up white light. We see them in a rainbow: red, orange, yellow, green, blue, indigo and violet,

Magically, our bodies have seven 'chakras' that react and respond to these colours. The word chakra is derived from Sanskrit, meaning 'wheel', or 'circle of life'. They consist of seven main energy centres found in the body and is associated with a variety of colours, symbols and Hindu gods.

When our chakras are in balance they spin and transmit pure colours around our cells in a flourish of electromagnetic impulses travelling at the speed of light. When our chakras are spinning our body functions well.

They are located along the spine, starting at the base of the spine and running upwards to the crown of the head. Each chakra coincides with an endocrine gland in the physical body which produces hormones, and each chakra radiates a specific colour and energy.

When we are 'off colour' or ill, we are literally lacking a colour in the part of our body that is manifesting physical dis-ease. If we feel lacking any particular aspect of our life, we might choose to wear or have a specific colour around us.

For example, if we are planning to have an important conversation with somebody, or are about to give a speech, wearing a turquoise scarf or a tie enhances our communication skills. More about that later on.

chakra magic

Chakra 1 – The Base (or Root Chakra)

Its colour is red, and it is located at the perineum, or base of our spine. It is the Chakra closest to the earth. Its function is concerned with physical survival and security. This Chakra is associated with our large intestine and adrenal glands. It controls our fight or flight response.

Its message is, 'I exist'. Blockage may manifest as paranoia, fear, procrastination and defensiveness.

Chakra 2 – The Sacral (or Navel Chakra)

Its colour is orange, and it is located between the base of our spine and our navel. It is associated with our kidneys, bladder, circulatory system, reproductive organs and glands. It is concerned with emotion and represents desire, pleasure, sexuality, procreation and creativity.

This chakra says, 'I desire'. Blockage may manifest as emotional problems, compulsive or obsessive behaviour and sexual guilt.

Chakra 3 – The Solar Plexus

Its colour is yellow, and it is located a few inches above the navel in the solar plexus area. This chakra is concerned with our digestive system, pancreas, and adrenals. It is the seat of our emotional life. Feelings of personal power, laughter, joy and anger are associated with this centre.

The message of the third chakra is 'I control'. Blockage may manifest as anger, frustration, lack of direction or a sense of victimisation.

Chakra 4 – The Heart

Its colour is green, and it is located within our heart. It is the centre of love, compassion, harmony, and peace. This Chakra concerns our lungs, chest and breasts, heart, and thymus gland.

The green chakra says, 'I love'. Blockage can show itself as immune system, breast, chest, lung and heart problems, lack of compassion – or heartlessness.

Chakra 5 - The Throat

Its colour is blue or turquoise and it is located within the throat. It is the Chakra of communication, creativity, self-expression and judgement. It is associated with our throat, the thyroid and parathyroid glands.

The message of the throat chakra is 'I express'. Blockage can show up as throat and voice problems, creative blocks, dishonesty or general problems in communicating with others.

Chakra 6 – The Third Eye (or Brow Chakra)

Its colour is Indigo. It is located at the centre of our forehead and is concerned with inner vision, intuition and wisdom.

This chakra tells the world 'I am content with who I am.' Blockage may manifest as problems like lack of foresight, mental rigidity and depression.

Chakra 7 – The Crown

Its colour is violet, and it is at the top of our head. It is associated with the pituitary gland. It is concerned with information, understanding, acceptance and bliss. It aids our connection to the universe through our higher self.

For most of us the crown chakra develops fully by the time we reach maturity, and it connects us with the wisdom of the universe. It says, 'I am open to my higher self.' Blockage can manifest as psychological problems.

chakra healing

If we feel a problem in any of the areas described above, it is good to wear something of that colour. For example, a sore throat might improve if you wrap a blue or turquoise scarf around your neck. If you have a difficult situation, where you will need strength to succeed, wear something red. Even if it is only your socks!

We may have heard the phrase 'your chakras are out of balance' but Diane Malaspina, PhD, a yoga medicine therapeutic specialist, says she prefers to think of chakras as out of balance versus blocked. She explains it like this:

'When a chakra is low in energy, you'll have difficulty expressing the particular qualities associated with that chakra. When a chakra is overactive, the qualities are a dominant force in the person's life. This can have both physical and emotional effects.

For example, the first chakra is about security, survival, and the foundation of our life. If it's underactive, it can show up as depression and insecurity. If there's too much energy, it can show up as fearlessness without precaution or hoarding because you need more to feel secure.'

life should be an upward progression

In an ideal world, and in some more primitive societies than our own, our lives as humans move naturally upwards through the chakras. Understanding their energies can help us to cope with the intricacies of life.

If we took more time to recognise the naturally developing stages of our body energy, our progression, as human beings, towards our higher selves would create a much more peaceful and harmonious society.

As **new-born babies** we are concerned solely with the basic tribal need for survival. Hunger and pain make us protest out loud. When we are happy, we smile and laugh. Our **red chakra** dominates, and it expresses itself loudly and simply – 'I need!'.

As **toddlers** we gradually grow away from our dependent babyhood state, we find our feet and start to acknowledge other people around us. At about the age of two we are keen to state our place in the world – this is me and this is who I am! 'I want!' is the cry of the **orange chakra**.

Our **yellow chakra** develops in our early **childhood**, and we start to reach out to the world. We love to make friends with other children and see other humans and pets as fellow creatures who we might be able to bargain with to get what we want. We still like to exercise our personal power, but we can be kind as well. 'I want you to be my friend,' is our yellow chakra expressing itself.

By the **teenage** years our **green, or heart chakra** starts to develop, and our bodies become ready to experience love. It is a great pity that in conventional society our most important years at school coincide with our sexual awakening. 'I love you,' is the cry of the heart chakra.

Teenage angst and frustrations start to fade when, as **young adults**, we should have learned how to express our knowledge and inner feelings. Our **blue chakra** wakens up and we tell the world 'I understand.'

Ideally by the time we reach **middle age** we are calm and secure with where and who we are in life. We are able to cope with life's ups and downs and can recognise that everyone is entitled to be themselves. We are not all the same. 'I accept' is the voice of the **indigo chakra**.

As **old age** approaches our **violet chakra** dominates. In more primitive societies the elders are revered and respected. Their wisdom is sought, and they are consulted often by the younger humans around them. They are the teachers.

It is sad that, in the hurried rough and tumble of today's fast living society, our senior citizens are often cast aside and neglected. Their voice calls 'I can teach', but too often their wisdom remains un-shared.

Children who regularly mix with older people see improvements to their language development, reading and social skills, something that is most easily achieved at 'intergenerational care' centres highlighted in the UK TV Channel 4 series *Old People's Home for 4 Year Olds*, says a report by United for All Ages.

Recognising and understanding the function of our chakras will help us and those around us to live happy, more fulfilled lives.

CHAPTER TWENTY
the magic of colour

soul colours

Colour resonates with our soul. Colour is all around, but how many of us realise how it can affect our daily lives and wellbeing? Colour is the visible part of the electromagnetic spectrum.

Our bodies take in colour through the eyes, the skin, through the food we eat and drink, and through our subconscious awareness.

The colours around us affect our moods. Hospital wards are often painted pale green – a relaxing and calming colour, whereas a schoolroom painted bright yellow will keep the students alert and encourage creative thinking.

Sunlight contains every colour of the spectrum – we see that when it is 'split' through a prism. Without sunlight, life on earth as we know it could not exist. Research has showed that light is stored in the DNA and is also the great communicator of the body, regulating the trillions of metabolic processes that occur naturally every second of the day during our whole lives.

Which colours have YOU got around your home? Try to fill your home with the colours that make you happy. Don't go with this season's colours, go with your heart. You don't have to go mad and change your entire colour scheme. Look for new cushion covers, throws, or a bunch of flowers in your chosen shade. Bring colours into your life and you invite better health to come along too!

the colours you wear

If you wear red...

Red symbolises a basic, vital force and you are impulsive, excitable and energetic. You are ambitious and like things to happen quickly. You like to be the best in everything you do. You are courageous and extroverted but can be irritable and bad tempered if you don't get your own way. This 'red' energy is best used in creativity or leadership – we all know about 'power dressing' and wearing red indicates a strong personality. Wearing red helps to heal the red chakra.

If you wear pink...

You have an affectionate, loving nature, which makes you sympathetic and understanding. You may, however, lack willpower and can be childlike in behaviour. You might need a great deal of support from others so you must learn to accept and love yourself. If you become more self-reliant you will attract and give out the feelings of warmth and love that you desire.

If you wear orange...

Orange is the colour of practicality and creativity. You are competent, self-oriented and impatient. You are also independent, an organizer and self-motivated. Your energy levels are high, and you are sometimes restless. You have a forceful will and tend to be active and competitive. You are also excitable and can seek domination over the others. If you feel you are lacking something, but you don't know what, orange will strengthen your sacral chakra

If you wear yellow…

Bright yellow represents spontaneity and communication. You are active, inspiring and like to investigate. You have an interesting and stimulating personality. Wearing yellow shows that you love the new and modern and it also brings a feeling of joy into your life because it stimulates your solar plexus.

If you wear green…

You are possibly a cautious person and not inclined to trust others easily. You are an observer in life and kind, although you don't like to get involved more than you have to. A quiet life suits you best, but perhaps you could be bolder in expressing your feelings. Green is the colour of the heart chakra and wearing it may help you to open your heart.

If you wear blue …

The colour blue is often seen as calming and conservative, but it can also be associated with intensity - think of a bright autumn sky, or sincerity - there's a reason we say someone is 'true blue'. Wearing blue may help you if you must have a difficult conversation or make a speech.

If you wear violet…

You have a sensitive, compassionate nature so you can be easily imposed upon and should be careful to pick friends who are as sensitive as you are. To be happy, work where you feel needed.

If you wear purple…

You are intuitive with deep feelings and high aspirations. You are interested in the best of everything, including your friends. Lesser mortals do not interest you or enter your scheme of things except where necessary. You can appear arrogant – so try to make more time for listening.

If you wear white…

White contains all the other colours in the spectrum, showing that you have a positive, well-balanced and optimistic personality. You may seek a simplified lifestyle free from outside pressures.

If you wear grey…

You are very much an individual. People may see you as self-sufficient because you have excellent self-control and like to remain uninvolved. But you can isolate yourself, which can lead to loneliness. You may be passive because you feel stressed and overburdened. If so take a break.

If you wear brown…

Brown clothing suggests an honest, down-to-earth person who likes a structured lifestyle. A lover of the best things life has to offer, you are a sensuous type, appreciating good food, drink and company. Brown is the colour of Mother Earth, but it can also hide your personality.

If you wear black …

You are strong-willed, opinionated and disciplined. But don't be too inflexible and independent. Black represents renunciation and those who always wear black might want to renounce everything out of a stubborn protest.

CHAPTER TWENTY-ONE
soul assistants

Connecting to the higher energy of the Universe means that we don't have to shoulder life's burdens alone.

A dear friend, when she came to my son's funeral, brought me a book about angels. She told me they would bring me comfort and indeed I did read it, from cover to cover. But my pain was so deep that I felt very distant from those heavenly beings and often I put the book aside, longing for the physical loss of my beautiful son. I missed being with him so much.

It was only when cancer struck and I was faced with the terrifying thought that I may not live to see my little granddaughter grow up that I searched again for spiritual help and found Nina. She helped me to believe again in the divine power of Angels and taught me a mantra 'If I can't fix this myself, I just hand it over to the Universe.'

angels – our universal helpers

Every religion encourages us to connect with a higher energy and their scriptures describe messengers from above who carry out tasks that they are assigned to perform on Earth.

When they visit Earth, angels may be in either human or heavenly form. They may visit in disguise, looking just like human beings, or they might appear as they've been popularly depicted in art, as creatures with human faces and powerful wings, often shining with light from within.

Angels are not just here with advice about lofty or complicated matters, they can help with mundane things as well such as finding lost items or exactly the right gift for your elderly aunt's birthday. So next time you are looking for a space to park your car ask the parking angels to find you one!

angelic visit

Nina could actually see angels. She told us about her friend Diana Cooper, who would be running a seminar on angels in Edinburgh and who had been visited by an angel when she was at her lowest ebb. I went to look at Diana's web site and found she had a most remarkable story:

'When I was 42, I was getting divorced and was at absolute rock bottom. There was no way to turn so I called out to the universe for help. I shouted, 'If there's anything out there, show me – and you've got one hour.' Immediately a beautiful six-foot-tall golden angel stood in front of me and pulled me out of my physical body. We flew together and it showed me many things. Finally, we flew together over a hall full of people with rainbow auras and it told me I was on the platform for I was to be a spiritual teacher. When it brought me back it was exactly one hour later.'

Sometime later, three angels appeared in front of her and gave her information about the angelic realms. She wrote a book about what they told her called *New Light on Angels* and it was published immediately and became a world-wide success. This was the first of over 30 books in 27 languages. Diana Cooper has inspired hundreds of thousands of people to fulfil their spiritual potential.

I have since met Diana Cooper several times, at workshops or seminars, and every time she walks onto a stage, or into a room she brings radiant light with her.

Like Nina, her message is always clear. Angels are all around us, ready to help with difficulties and guide us to find our higher self. All we have to do is to ask them.

beautiful beings of light

Whether we can see them or not, angels are always around us and are waiting to assist us whenever we ask. There are angels for every task that we need help with, from finding lost keys to organising a parking space.

I went to dozens of classes, talks and workshops about angels while I was in the process of healing, and to anyone who told me they don't exist I would say, you may not believe in angels, but they believe in you. I had nothing to lose and everything to gain when I learned to welcome these heavenly beings into my life. They have brought me nothing but light.

Everyone has at least one Guardian Angel. They are heavenly spirits assigned by God to watch over each of us during our lives. They are present to welcome us at birth and will travel with us to our next life when we die.

the powers of archangels

Archangels are pretty much the highest ranking among the celestial beings and are found in many faiths. Michael and Gabriel are recognised in Judaism, Islam, the Baha'i Faith, and by most Christians. But Uriel and Raphael take their place also among these most powerful beings. Each of the four Archangels has powerful specific energies that we call upon when we need help.

Michael is the highest Archangel and when he arrives, a sense of protection and warmth immediately empower us. Protection, truth, integrity, courage, and strength are characteristics of this bold and mighty angel. He shines with a vivid blue light and, if we need courage, we can close our eyes and visualise our self bathed in his powerful blue energy.

Archangel Gabriel often shows up bearing an important message. That's because she is the top angelic messenger of God and she is surrounded by a shining white light. Often appearing in dreams to those that need help with communication skills, she can provide purity, fulfilment and direction in achieving our life's goal. We know that Gabriel was chosen to tell Mary that she would give birth to Jesus.

I called on Raphael's help a lot in my path towards healing. His name means *'He who heals'* in Hebrew, and he is surrounded with a glowing green light. Raphael works quickly to heal the mind, spirit, and body of all who ask so they can enjoy good health and peace. His presence is sometimes announced with a witty physical action, such as a book falling from a shelf.

Archangel Uriel shows us the difference between good and evil and he is there when we need to make the right decisions, solve a problem or resolve a conflict. Uriel brings wisdom to all that ask. Purple and gold are Uriel's colours, representing courage, wisdom and mercy. By asking for Archangel Uriel's help we can let go of resentment and bitterness.

auras and energy

We all have a field of energy that surrounds our body, called an aura. Most people are not able to see auras, but we can often feel this energy. The colour of our aura reflects our physical, emotional, and spiritual health. Someone who is healthy, self-confident, and positive tends to have a bright, light aura that other people can sense, even if they can't see it. When we describe someone as having a 'magnetic personality' we are in fact feeling their aura.

We know that laughing can be infectious, and we enjoy being with a cheery person. Their good energy radiates around them. But we have all met people who exude darkness. We might begin to feel depressed and drained, and if we don't get away, we can start to feel dejected as well.

But if I find myself beside someone who is clearly down in the dumps, even if we are just standing in a queue or sitting on a bus. I like to make an effort to make them smile by saying something cheerful and often that seems to unlock something within them, and they will tell me what is on their mind. If I'm not in a hurry I quite often get a potted life story from a stranger. I always listen, because I know the person will invariably go away sounding much happier, and that makes me happy too. By deliberately expanding my energy field, I am able to raise their energy.

Some say that when our chakras are spinning well our good energy bubbles out and surrounds us with shining light. Diana Cooper and my friend Nina both had auras which shone so brightly that they literally brightened up the room. Everyone could feel the burst of good energy when they walked in.

shining out

I loved going to 'Angel Fairs' when I lived in town and sometimes, I would travel further afield if there was a particular person I wanted to meet. I went to several in London and met some amazing and inspiring people. Even if there was nobody particularly well-known taking part, it was always such a joyful and uplifting experience, filled with lovely sights, scents and sounds.

Once I was wandering round a 'Mind, Body and Spirit' event with a friend when we came across a stand offering to photograph our auras. My friend went to have hers done and her hands were placed on two sensitive pads that could 'read' the electro-magnetic field that surrounded her body. At the end she was given a photograph. It showed her body surrounded by colours, gorgeous purples and reds with a hint of vibrant green and turquoise.

The interpretation, that she was passionate, unconventional, determined, and loyal fitted her personality perfectly! When I sat for mine, it was filled with blues and greens. I was told that although I was creative, I must learn not to hold myself back. I could be too sensitive and should make an effort to connect more with the world.

Well, that was an eye opener! Following that advice did not come easily but nevertheless I did my best not to sabotage my chances of success with negative thinking. I realised I could sometimes appear aloof and judgemental and that was a good lesson too.

energy is really all there is!

The World we live in is all made of light. There is no beginning or end to what we are. Everything is made of energy, and we can never separate from it.

We are all swimming in this light that creates the entire world we see. Energy moves freely and it cannot be extinguished.

A wonderful set of books about the power of energy is the Celestine Prophecy series by James Redfield. Easy to read, I learned so much from them.

In the form of exciting adventure novels, they teach twelve spiritual 'insights', such as recognising synchronicity and the control dramas that we as humans, use to manipulate those around us!

Drawing on ancient wisdom, James Redfield tells us how to make connections among the events happening in our life right now and lets us see what is going to happen to us in the years to come. The story is a gripping one of adventure and discovery, but it is also a guidebook that has the power to crystallize your perceptions of why you are where you are in life and to direct your steps with a new energy and optimism as you head into tomorrow.

Once we recognise and learn to balance the energies inside our bodies and outside of them, in mind, body and spirit, we set ourselves on the path to perfect wholeness, or health, and it changes our lives for the better, forever!

SECTION THREE

FOOD

FOR LIGHT & LIFE

LIGHT-BRINGING 'SUPERFOODS'

The term 'superfood' is often avoided by nutritionists since it implies that the food in question has superpowers that will cure whatever ails you. I'm not saying that superfoods are a cure-all, but they do contain more nutrition than your average food. We know for sure that eating a diet full of healthy foods is gives us many health benefits and a decreased risk of chronic disease.

Avocados

Avocados are high in several important nutrients, many of which are lacking in modern diets. They contain no cholesterol, and are full of protein, 'good' oil, and carbohydrate levels. They also provide Vitamin C to boost the immune system, Vitamin B thiamine and riboflavin, needed to boost metabolic rate and potassium to improve our blood circulation.

They also provide a rich source of vitamin E which promotes white blood cell activity, especially in the production of T-cells which are the white cells which fight infections.

Beans

Legumes like beans, peas and lentils are rich in fibre and saponins - compounds that block tumour growth by inhibiting DNA synthesis.

As well as being high in fibre, beans score low on the glycaemic index, a ranking of foods based on how they affect blood sugar. Because of the fibre and protein, the carbs in beans get absorbed at a slower rate over a longer time. That helps keep your blood sugar steady—one reason beans can help keep diabetes at bay.

Brown Rice

Brown rice has a nutty flavour and is chewier than white rice. It is much more nutritious being unrefined.
It has long been a valuable addition to the diet in cases of cancer, obesity, diabetes, nervous disorders, depression and even insomnia. It is effective in maintaining a healthy heart, brain, and digestive system and, good news for osteoporosis sufferers, it also maintains strong bones.

Brown rice cooking instructions:

Cooking brown rice is easy, but it takes a little more water and time than regular white rice.
Use 1 mug brown rice to 2 mugs water and a pinch of salt. If you've time, soak first in cold water for about an hour. Soaking the brown rice before cooking helps soften the tough outer layer of the rice grains, making it more digestible and releasing enzymes that make it more nutritious. Then rinse in a sieve until the water runs clear. This helps remove loose starch so the rice will be less sticky. Drain the rice thoroughly and put in a saucepan. Add the water and salt. Bring to the boil. Stir once, then cover the pot with a tight-fitting lid and reduce the heat to a very low simmer or it will boil over.

Cook for 30-40 minutes or until most of the water has been absorbed. Start checking at 30 minutes to prevent the rice from burning.

Turn off the heat and let the rice sit in the covered saucepan for at least 10 minutes so it absorbs the remaining liquid. When you're ready to serve, remove the lid and fluff the rice with a fork to separate the grains.

Chia Seeds

Chia seeds are the tiny black seeds from the Salvia Hispanica plant. When soaked, the seeds may promote bone health, be good for your heart and lower blood pressure. They improve blood sugar management and reduce the risk of diabetes as well as improving digestive health due to their poly-unsaturated fat content, high fibre levels and anti-inflammatory properties. Soak for at least twenty minutes before eating, in water or milk.

Congee

Congee is a famously healing porridge from the Far East. that is easy on the stomach and offers a gentle and highly digestible source of nutrients. Congee has long been used as a traditional breakfast food and digestive remedy.

How to make congee

¾ cup of brown rice
9 cups water
1 tsp fine sea or rock salt

It can be made in a pot or a slow cooker.

Add the water and rice and bring to a boil. If you're using an ordinary pot, leave lid partially open so that it can vent steam.

Cook on low, stirring occasionally for about 1-½ hours If you have enough time, you can let it cook for 2-6 hours.

Tip: Make with stock for a savoury taste and add garlic, sliced spring onions, sprouts, grated carrots, or ghee.

If you like something sweet, try adding coconut milk, pure vanilla, chopped nuts, raisins or cranberries, cinnamon and a drizzle of honey or maple syrup.

Fermented Foods

Fermented foods are incredibly good for us! They are literally teeming with lactobacillus bacteria, predigesting the ingredients that they are made of, and transforming them into superfoods for our trillions of gut bacteria, as well as adding incredibly important probiotics.

Probiotics have been shown to improve symptoms in IBS, traveller's diarrhoea and the duration of antibiotic associated diarrhoea. There is emerging evidence that probiotics may improve cholesterol levels in people with type II diabetes and could also play a role in benefitting cold or flu outcomes during stressful periods.

Literally hundreds of vegetables are suitable for fermentation but most popular is *Sauerkraut – literally 'sour cabbage'. Sauerkraut does lots of good things for our body, especially our gut and there are multiple reasons sauerkraut may help with weight loss. For one thing, sauerkraut is low in calories and high in fibre, which can help you feel full longer. This can help reduce the amount of food you eat in a day without leaving you feeling hungry.

Obesity affects more than 60% of adults and children in the Western world and is associated with increased risks of heart disease, digestive problems, and type 2 diabetes.

The probiotics in sauerkraut may also decrease fat absorption. These studies are still in the preliminary stages, and the results have yet to be replicated in humans. However, these early studies are promising and point to probiotics being key to weight loss.

More about sauerkraut later on in this section.

Feta Cheese

Feta is lower in fat and higher in calcium than many other cheeses, and because it's not traditionally made from cow's milk, but with milk from sheep and goats, it's also easier to digest. When eaten in moderation, feta helps you maintain healthy teeth and bones.

Feta cheese also has high levels of phosphorus. Consuming phosphorus and calcium together has been linked to improved bone density and osteoporosis prevention.

Feta may also assist with weight management because it contains a fatty acid known as conjugated linoleic acid (CLA). Experimental studies have shown that CLA can help reduce body fat. These studies also show that CLA can help improve your body composition in the long term. Feta cheese is a good source of essential vitamins and minerals.

It is typically made from the milk of sheep and goats. One of the oldest cheeses in the world, it's known for a rich aroma and slightly sour taste.

NB: Although feta cheese is a good source of essential vitamins and minerals, the high sodium content in feta cheese may cause complications with certain medical conditions.

Flax Seed Oil

This is a super superfood because it works to fight three big health concerns - internal cleansing, cardiovascular disease, and cancers.

They also provide calcium, iron, niacin, phosphorous and vitamin E. Most importantly for vegetarians, they are also a rich source of Omega-3 fatty acids, an Essential Fatty Acid or EFA. These are needed by the human body to maintain normal function. They carry light into our cells.

Just one small serving of this delicious 'miracle' food gives us fantastic protection against cancer and heart disease. Flax seed oil also lowers our cholesterol and has been successful in reversing kidney damage caused by lupus.

We can buy whole or more easily absorbed ground flax seeds in health-food shops and supermarkets. They can be sprinkled over cereals and hot dishes or made into a nourishing tea (see the recipe section). Be sure to drink plenty of water – I mean LOTS of water, otherwise the seeds absorb too much moisture from the gut, resulting in constipation. The seeds can also be sprouted and used in salads and sandwiches.

Flax contains lignans, which can block or suppress cancerous changes. Countless studies prove that flax seed lignans can significantly reduce the incidence of hormone related cancers such as breast, endometrial and prostate cancers and several studies confirm that flaxseed can be a cholesterol-lowering agent.

Flax Seed (Linseed) Tea **

Drinking 2-3 mugs of linseed tea per day between meals can be very helpful for digestive problems, stiff aching joints or as part of a gentle detox plan.

Linseeds (or flaxseeds) are rich in mucilage that coats, soothes and hydrates your digestive tract which in turn, supports the hydration of your entire body.

In a pan, add 2 tablespoons of golden linseeds to 1.5 litres of water and bring to the boil. Switch off the heat and leave the mixture to stand for 12 hours or overnight. Reheat and simmer for an hour with the lid on the pan. Strain the seeds off and keep the remaining thick liquid in the fridge. To make a tea with it, dilute a 50/50 mixture of linseed tea and fresh hot water.

** From *'Cellular Awakening'* by Barbara Wren

Flax Seed Tea – 'The Cheat Method'

This method is good for those who must go out top work, or who would find making the traditional method another stress – remember, stress = dehydration!
So, for the cheat method, take a one-pint stainless steel flask or glass-lined thermos. pop in a tablespoon of linseeds, fill the flask to the top with boiling filtered water, put the lid on and leave overnight. Sip throughout the day, shaking first and drinking the seeds whole for their cleansing ability.

Garlic

Garlic is one of the oldest food flavourings: archaeological records have found that it was used even in Neolithic times, more than eight thousand years ago. But garlic was used as a wound antiseptic and cure for infections in both World War I and World War II. Ancient Greeks left garlic at the crossroads as an offering to the goddess of wilderness and childbirth Hecate.

Garlic has loads of benefits to the body. Apart from providing vitamins and minerals it is highly effective against parasites and fungal infections, as well as disorders of the gut caused by Salmonella and food poisoning. Raw garlic may be mashed and mixed with coconut oil to make an effective ointment against athlete's foot!

Recent studies are proving that garlic works in both prevention and treatment, of cancer. Compounds in garlic appear to increase the activity of immune cells which fight cancer and indirectly help break down cancer-causing substances. These compounds also help block carcinogens from entering cells and slow tumour development.

People who eat raw or cooked garlic regularly, cut their risk of stomach, oesophagus, pancreatic and breast cancers by about a half compared with those who eat no garlic. They also cut their risk of colorectal cancer by as much as two-thirds. Diallyl sulphide, a component of garlic oil, has also been shown to render carcinogens in the liver inactive. If you suffer from an autoimmune disease (a growing worldwide epidemic), you need garlic in your diet! With benefits such as these, who cares about having smelly breath!

Ghee

Ghee is made from butter, treated with low heat until the water evaporates, leaving behind milk solids. The solids are skimmed off or strained. What remains is only clarified liquid fat known as ghee. It has long been popular in the culinary traditions of the Middle East and also used with herbal medication as a part of Ayurveda, a centuries-old form of alternative medicine in India.

Ginger

Ginger is a fantastic alkaliser and nibbling a small piece of root ginger is better than an indigestion tablet for the stomach.

Sipping a cup of hot water with a slice of fresh root ginger in it helps to banish post - chemotherapy nausea and even helps fight flu and the common cold.

Green food

Raw green foods like sprouted seeds, broccoli, baby spinach, herbs and salad leaves are chlorophyll-rich and enzyme-rich 'super foods'. They take the burden off an overloaded system and allow it to recover. The high chlorophyll content of sprouts, salad greens and herbs act in two ways, detoxing and rejuvenating at the same time.

Honey

Honey is a well-known antiseptic, used externally, and when eaten it has amazing antioxidant properties. Unprocessed honey helps treat skin infections, helps wounds heal, and improves dandruff and itchy scalp. In emergency, honey can be spread over burns to protect the area until medical help can be reached. Honey is an old-fashioned remedy for coughs and sore throats.

Kale

Kale is a member of the cabbage (Brassica) family and is often labelled a superfood because it is so high in nutrients per calorie. Kale is also low in fat and high in fibre, making it a great addition to almost any diet for the brilliant nutritional and health benefits it provides.

One cup of raw kale (20.6g) provides 7.2 calories, 0.6g of protein, 0.9g of carbohydrates, and 0.3g of fat. Kale is a great source of vitamins A, K, and C, as well as potassium and calcium.

Kefir

Kefir is a cultured fermented milk drink, traditionally made with goats milk and living kefir 'grains' which are combinations of living good gut bacteria and yeast. You can't manufacture a kefir grain – grains only grow from other grains.

The first drinking kefir was made by the inhabitants of the Black Caucasus Mountains in Russia, thousands of years ago, but no one knows where the first kefir grain came from – its origins are lost in the mists of time!

Millet

Millet is one of the earliest cultivated grains and it is naturally gluten-free. It looks like tiny corn kernels and costs about a quarter of what you would pay for quinoa, making it among the more economical gluten-free grains available. Some people liken the slightly sweet flavour to corn. But the fluffy texture of cooked millet, similar to mashed potatoes or steamed rice, distinguishes it from other whole grains, such as chewy barley or buckwheat. Similar to those whole grains, though, millet has a slightly nutty flavour, which toasting enhances.

Mushroom Magic

Mushrooms are high in antioxidants, the chemicals that get rid of free radicals – things which harm our cells, potentially leading to cancer. Mushrooms contain almost no fat, sugar or salt but they do provide dietary fibre.

Mushrooms contain selenium, a mineral that is not present in most fruits and vegetables. Selenium prevents inflammation and reduces growth of some tumours.

The vitamin D in mushrooms can also inhibit the growth of cancer cells. They are also rich in B vitamins: riboflavin, niacin, and pantothenic acid, making them good for heart health and the nervous system.

In Japan, mushrooms, especially Shiitake, have been valued for their anti-cancer properties, because they stimulate the activity of the body's T-cells.

The healthiest mushrooms to look for include:
Lion's Mane, Reishi, Cordyceps, Chaga, Turkey Tail, Shiitake, Maitake and Oyster
Medicinal mushrooms are nutritional powerhouses with a myriad of health benefits including the following:

- Provide immune support
- Full of antioxidants
- Support a healthy inflammation response
- Help to balance blood sugar
- Support brain health and cognition
- Support the nervous system
- Increase energy and stamina

Nuts

Nuts are one of the prehistoric survival foods of our ancestral hunter-gatherers. Recent research found that eating more than 5 ounces of nuts a week cut heart-attack deaths in women by 40% and helped prevent deadly irregular heartbeats in men.

Oats

Oats are one of the healthiest grains and are incredibly nutritious. Oatmeal is very filling and may help you lose weight. They are a good source of 'slow release' carbohydrates (Low G I) that help to keep your blood glucose (sugar) level on an even keel. The carbs in oats are mostly starches and fibre. Oats are a good source of beta glucan, a unique, soluble fibre linked to multiple health benefits such as lowering cholesterol levels.

Oats pack more protein and fat than most other grains. This is in the form of avenin, a protein-like gluten, although research has shown that most people with coeliac disease can safely eat avenin.

Oats offer high amounts of many vitamins and minerals, such as manganese, phosphorus, copper, B vitamins, iron, selenium, magnesium, and zinc. Oats are the only dietary source of powerful antioxidants known as 'avenanthramides' as well as ferulic acid and phytic acid.

Oats have also recently been shown to exhibit anti-inflammatory, antiproliferative, and anti-itching activity, which may provide additional protection against coronary heart disease, colon cancer, and skin irritation.

Pine Nuts

Pine Nut Kernels are a great source of Vitamin E, Vitamin B1, Potassium, Iron, Zinc and Manganese.

They are delicious sprinkled onto salads or lightly toast to bring out their flavour and add extra crunchiness!

Quinoa

This ancient seed (pronounced KEEN-WA) is gluten free because it is not a grain. It cooks quickly and has a delightful, slightly crunchy, texture. It's got a lot of the amino acid lysine, so it provides a more complete protein than cereal grains.

On its own it has a bitter flavour so cook it in vegetable stock, add fresh herbs, garlic or onion, or toast it before boiling.

Sauerkraut

Learning to make your own sauerkraut is a fantastic way to give yourself and your family many extra health benefits!

Nutrition - In addition to its other benefits, sauerkraut is a source of several key nutrients, including:

- o Vitamin C
- o Vitamin K1
- o Iron
- o Folate
- o Manganese
- o Copper
- o Potassium

Simple Sauerkraut Recipe

Sauerkraut is the original superfood, long before that word was even used. A traditionally fermented product, consisting of two simple ingredients, salt and cabbage, sauerkraut has been produced for over 4,000 years.

1 tightly packed white or red cabbage
1 tablespoon of fine sea or rock salt for every 500g of cabbage
1 tsp caraway seeds and / or dill for extra flavour

Take off 2 or 3 of the tough outer cabbage leaves and set aside; cut out the central hard stalk. Shred the cabbage finely with a sharp knife, (or use a food processor with a slicing blade attachment)

Place in a large mixing bowl and sprinkle the shredded cabbage with salt, add caraway seeds and / or dill if you like the taste Massage the salt well into cabbage until the juices run freely when a handful is squeezed – at least five or more minutes.

Place massaged cabbage into a wide-topped Kilner – type jar (Mason jar in US). Leave a gap at the top for a weight. Place 2 or 3 of the large outer leaves on top and press down until the juice creeps out over them. Place a weight on top of cabbage (I use a glass ramekin, but you can just use a smaller jar filled with dried beans). Cover jars with cheesecloth held on with elastic band' Check every 24 hours making sure no air has got under the top layer or it will go mouldy and need discarding.

Ferment for 3-10 days. Remove cheesecloth, replace with the Kilner jar lids. Place in fridge and eat some every day.

Salt Brine for Preserving

Cabbages have so much moisture in them already that they create their own brine with just some salt, but I keep a bottle filled with fermenting brine (using 1 tablespoon of sea salt to 1 pint of filtered/spring water) and keep it for preserving other surplus vegetables. Carrots, celery, broccoli, asparagus, squash, beetroot, peppers, and cauliflower can all be fermented.

While you can ferment virtually any vegetable you like, you'll want to make sure the ingredients in your jar are roughly the same shape and size. This will ensure that they all ferment at the same rate.

Pack your fermenting jars with the vegetables and cover them with brine. Keep everything submerged, and store in a cool cupboard or pantry.

Sesame Seeds

Sesame seeds are packed with protein, iron, zinc, magnesium, calcium and phytic acid while being low in carbohydrates. They also contain substances that may help lower cholesterol levels, and are a well-known source of vitamin E plus omega-6 and monounsaturated fats. These can help to prevent furring of the arteries as well as boost the elasticity of the skin. As an added bonus, sesame seeds are thought to aid digestion, to stimulate blood circulation and help the nervous system.

Shiitake Mushrooms

The shiitake is an incredible edible mushroom native to East Asia. Because of its health benefits, it has been considered a medicinal mushroom in traditional herbal medicine, mentioned in books written thousands of years ago. Japanese scientists have found that Shiitake extract appears to restore melanoma-reactive T cells, an important and non-invasive aspect of cancer treatment.

Shiitake mushrooms contain many chemical compounds that protect our DNA from oxidative damage, which is partly why they're so beneficial. Lentinan, for example, heals chromosome damage caused by anticancer treatments.

They are also a unique plant, because they contain all eight essential amino acids, along with a type of essential fatty acid called linoleic acid. Linoleic acid helps with weight loss and building muscle. It also has bone-building benefits, improves digestion, and reduces food allergies and sensitivities.

Shiitakes have a meaty texture and woodsy flavour, making them the perfect addition to soups, salads, meat dishes and stir-fries.

Sprouted Seeds

You can buy inexpensive sprouters, but all you need to sprout your own superfood is a large glass jar or jug, a square of muslin and an elastic band!

First choose what to sprout, remembering that some will take longer than others. Small similarly sized seeds may be sprouted together to make a tasty salad mixture. Try fenugreek, mustard, and alfalfa. A tablespoon of seeds will provide a surprising quantity of sprouts.

Place the seeds in the jar or jug, wash with cold water and leave them to soak overnight, covered with fresh water. Rinse again, drain off the water, stretch the muslin over the neck of the jar and secure with the elastic band. Rinse the seeds twice daily draining thoroughly. Keep in a warm place, but not too hot, in the light, but out of sunlight.

Alfalfa and poppy seeds will be ready in a couple of days; beans and lentils take a little longer. Once you have tasted these lovely fresh, healthy sprouts you will find lots of ways to use them in salads and stir-fries. No preparation or cooking is needed - most sprouts can be eaten raw ***. They are highly nutritious: sprouts are simply bursting with vitamins and minerals. They are also a good source of chlorophyll which is said to have anti-bacterial and anti-inflammatory properties.

Raw sprouts are an excellent source of plant enzymes, making them very easy to digest and in fact donate enzymes to help us digest other foods more efficiently - they're a real superfood!

*** Always cook shop-bought beansprouts, the water they are sprouted in may not necessarily be pure.

Tofu

Tofu is to soya milk as cheese is to dairy milk, but it is a low-fat option. Cheese is made when milk separates into curds and whey, and tofu is made when soya milk separates into curds and whey. So, tofu is the curd of soya milk – it is sometimes called bean curd. On it's own it is fairly tasteless, but marinated or cooked along with garlic, ginger or other flavour-rich foods it is delicious.

Tofu is rich in high-quality protein and contains all eight essential amino acids. It is also a good source of B-vitamins and iron. A four-ounce serving of tofu contains just 6 grams of fat. It is low in saturated fat and contains no cholesterol.

Turmeric

Turmeric has been used for thousands of years in both cooking and as a medicinal herb. It contains curcumin, which has powerful anti-inflammatory and antioxidant properties. Its effects are enhanced by black pepper.

It can reduce inflammation by blocking enzymes and other proteins that create an inflammatory response in the body.

It may support your joints and protect them from wear and tear. This includes easing symptoms of arthritis like joint movement and stiffness, according to a 2016 study in Journal of Medicinal Food.

It can ease digestion problems – curcumin can help support gut health, including relieving excess gas, abdominal pain, and bloating.

Yogurt

Yogurt is made by the bacterial fermentation of milk, and humans have consumed it for hundreds of years. It can be made from all types of milk including plant milk, which is ideal for anyone worried about consuming dairy products.

The bacteria used to make yogurt are called "yogurt cultures," which ferment lactose, the natural sugar found in milk. This process produces lactic acid, a substance that causes milk proteins to curdle, giving yogurt its unique flavour and texture.

It's very nutritious and eating it regularly may boost several aspects of your health. For example, yogurt is high in B vitamins, particularly vitamin B12 and riboflavin, both of which may protect against heart disease. It also contains phosphorus, magnesium, calcium and potassium. These minerals are essential for several biological processes, such as regulating blood pressure, metabolism, and bone health. It has been found to reduce the risk of osteoporosis and helps in weight management.

Although cancer is mentioned frequently in this shopping list, many other ailments such as diabetes and heart disease can be improved when these foods are included in the diet.

Even if you are undergoing treatment, none of these foodstuffs will interfere with the programme. In fact they will flood your body with health-affirming energy.

shopping for health

When we get ill it is easy to fall into despair and feel powerless. We can become afraid or confused and not know how we can help ourselves to get better. We worry that it will become very expensive when we look at costly supplements that promise to sort our health issues. Even if you only want to improve your family's chances of not getting ill, then this shopping list will be invaluable!

The good news is that many foods commonly found in our local shops contain disease -fighting properties. The following foods can all help stave off many disorders, including cancer.

There isn't a single element in a particular food that does all the work: The best thing to do is eat a variety of these foods. Even if you have been diagnosed with cancer, there are many nutritional ways you can improve your chances of recovery.

Although the shopping list is far from comprehensive it will set you on the path towards filling your basket with foods that will help to support your immune system.

Once you start to eat more fresh foods and less refined products you will notice subtle changes which herald more light coming into your body. Your skin will be brighter and clearer; your gut health will improve and any tendency towards constipation will lessen. You will have more energy and feel generally more optimistic.

Go on – try it and see, you will be glad you did!!!

SHOPPING LIST

To bring light to your menu

APPLES An apple a day may keep the oncologist away! Naturally occurring chemicals in apples slow the growth rate of human colon-cancer cells and liver-cancer cells. The anti-cancer effect is strongest in extracts made from unpeeled apples, which contain more antioxidant phytochemicals (plant chemicals containing substances that prevent or delay deterioration caused by oxygen).

APRICOT KERNELS contain laetrile (Vitamin B17) which actually destroys cancer cells. This potent substance is found in many other nuts & seeds, even apple pips, so eat them – they are good for you!

AVOCADOS are rich in glutathione, a powerful antioxidant that attacks free radicals in the body by blocking intestinal absorption of certain fats. They also supply even more potassium than bananas and are a strong source of beta-carotene. Scientists also believe that avocados may also be useful in treating viral hepatitis (a possible trigger for liver cancer), as well as other sources of liver damage.

BANANAS are a good source of potassium and vitamin B6, but they also encourage production of serotonin, the feel-good chemical compound which can help to defeat cancer.

BEANS are particularly rich in nutrients that may protect against cancer, and are a low-fat, high-protein alternative to meat. Broad beans contain lectin, a substance which can fight cancer. Even the humble baked bean helps in the anti-cancer journey, and is high in fibre and protein. But choose a brand with no added salt or sugar.

BEAN -SPROUTS contain resveratrol which is converted in the body to a known anti-cancer agent that can selectively target and destroy cancer cells. *NB: The trays of beansprouts bought at the shop may not be safe to eat raw so, to be sure, only use them in recipes where they are properly cooked.*

BROCCOLI, CABBAGE & CAULIFLOWER contain a chemical component called indole-3-carbinol that can combat breast cancer by converting a cancer-promoting oestrogen into a more protective variety. Broccoli, especially the florets, is also believed to aid in preventing some types of cancer, like colon, stomach, and rectal cancer. All cruciferous vegetables – broccoli, cauliflower, cabbage, kale and Brussels sprouts, contain two antioxidants, lutein and zeaxanthin that may help decrease prostate and other cancers.

CAYENNE, CHILLIS & JALAPENOS contain a chemical, capsaicin, which may neutralize certain cancer-causing substances (nitrosamines). Thanks to capsaicin, cayenne can be used to treat heart disease, fight cancer, clean the bloodstream and ward off diseases. Although, it is primarily used for improving blood flow, there are other benefits, when it comes to heart disease. Cayenne pepper has long been used in Native American medicine to remedy heart problems,

CHIA SEEDS are the tiny black seeds from the Salvia Hispanica plant. When soaked, the seeds may promote bone health, be good for your heart and lower blood pressure. They may improve blood sugar management and reduce the risk of diabetes as well as improving digestive health due to their poly-unsaturated fat content, high fibre levels and anti-inflammatory properties.

DARK CHOCOLATE contains ant-oxidants and minerals. It might help lower the risk of heart disease and helps the body to manufacture serotonin, the 'feel-good' chemical, in the brain and gut.

ESSENTIAL FATTY ACIDS or EFAs, are fatty acids that humans and other animals must ingest because the body requires them for good health but cannot synthesize them. The term 'essential fatty acid' refers to fatty acids required for biological processes but does not include the fats that only act as fuel. These bring light to our cells as well as a multitude of other health benefits.

FLAX SEEDS contain lignans, which may have an antioxidant effect and block or suppress cancerous changes. Flax is also high in omega-3 fatty acids, which are thought to protect against many cancers as well as heart disease.

GARLIC has immune-enhancing allium compounds that appear to increase the activity of immune cells that fight cancer. These substances (diallyl sulphides) also help block carcinogens from entering cells and slow tumour development. Diallyl sulphide, a component of garlic oil, but also found in onions, leeks and chives, has also been shown to render carcinogens in the liver inactive. Studies have shown that people who eat raw or cooked garlic regularly, face half the risk of stomach cancer and two-thirds the risk of colon and rectal cancer as people who eat little or none. It is believed garlic may help prevent stomach cancer because it has anti-bacterial effects against a bacterium, Helicobacter pylori, found in the stomach and known to promote cancer there.

GRAPEFRUITS contain monoterpenes, believed to help prevent cancer by sweeping carcinogens out of the body. Studies show that grapefruit may inhibit the proliferation of breast-cancer cells in vitro. They also contains vitamin C, beta-carotene, and folic acid.

However do check with your health advisor if you are taking certain prescription medicines as grapefruit may interfere with the effectiveness of some, such as statins and some heart or epilepsy drugs.

Red GRAPES contain bioflavonoids, which are powerful antioxidants that work as cancer preventives. Grapes are also a rich source of resveratrol, which inhibits the enzymes that can stimulate cancer-cell growth and suppress immune response. They also contain ellagic acid, a compound that blocks enzymes that are necessary for cancer cells; this appears to help slow the growth of tumours.

HERBS like Rosemary may help increase the activity of detoxification enzymes. An extract of rosemary, termed carnosol, has inhibited the development of both breast and skin tumours in animals, though we haven't found any studies done on humans. Other fresh herbs like parsley and basil have high levels of vitamin C and other beneficial properties when used as flavourings or infusions.

KALE has indoles, nitrogen compounds which may help stop the conversion of certain lesions to cancerous cells in oestrogen-sensitive tissues. In addition, isothiocyanates, phytochemicals found in kale, are thought to suppress tumour growth and block cancer-causing substances from reaching their targets.

LIQUORICE root has a chemical, glycyrrhizin, that blocks a component of testosterone and therefore may help prevent the growth of prostate cancer. (However, too much can lead to elevated blood pressure and diarrhoea, so beware.)

MILLET is the only grain which contains no acid. It is rich in phytate. This phytochemical appears to reduce colon and mammary gland cancer in animals – so may play a part in preventing breast cancer.

MUSHROOMS – There are a number of mushrooms that appear to help the body fight cancer and build the immune system – Shiitake, maitake, reishi, oyster and portobello have documented health benefits These mushrooms contain polysaccharides, especially Lentinan, a very powerful compound that helps in building immunity. They also have a protein called lectin, which attacks cancerous cells and prevents them from multiplying. These mushrooms can stimulate the production of interferon in the body. Extracts from mushrooms have been successfully tested in recent years in Japan as an adjunct to chemotherapy.

NUTS contain the antioxidants quercetin and kaempferol that may suppress the growth of cancers. Nuts and seeds contain copper, a trace element recognized as important in helping the body ward off colon cancer. A Brazil nut contains 80 micrograms of selenium, which is important for those with prostate cancer. If you are allergic to nuts, you may consider taking a selenium supplement

ORANGES & LEMONS contain limonene which stimulates cancer-killing immune cells like lymphocytes, that may also break down cancer-causing substances.

PINEAPPLE has a high manganese content, so is good for preventing osteoporosis and bone fractures, but it also contains an important cancer-fighting enzyme called bromelain**. This breaks down food and dead tissue and 'digests' protein quickly, a key factor in combating cancer. ** NB: Bromelain does not survive processing so must be obtained from fresh pineapples; tinned fruit or cartons of juice do not contain bromelain.

POTATOES contain chemicals that may block cancer. The skins are especially rich in chlorogenic acid which prevents cell mutations leading to cancer. They also contain potassium.

QUINOA – provides phyto-oestrogens. Women who eat the most phyto-oestrogenic foods are four times less likely to be diagnosed with breast cancer than those who eat the least. Two amino acids found in Quinoa, both of which are antioxidants, are Methionine and Cysteine. Methionine is a neutralizer of toxins. Cysteine helps combat cancer, metal toxicity, and skin problems. It promotes wound healing and stimulates the immune system.

RASPBERRIES and other berries contain many vitamins, minerals, plant compounds and antioxidants known as anthocyanins that may protect against cancer.

RED WINE has polyphenols (potent antioxidants) that may protect against various types of cancer. Also, the compound resveratrol is found in the grape skins. However, high alcohol intake has also been linked to breast cancer development, so as with all things, moderation is indicated. You might look for organic wines, but for those on a detox NO alcohol is best.

RICE – is a healthy alternative to potatoes or pasta, but brown rice is the one with outstanding health benefits: it contains lots of insoluble dietary fibre, which is crucial to good gut health and serves a major protective function in colon cancer. Researchers theorise that carcinogens are diluted by fluid, attracted and bound to the fibres, and then quickly excreted as the fibres pass through the gastrointestinal tract for elimination.

SEAWEED and other SEA VEGETABLES contain beta-carotene, protein, vitamin B12, fibre, and chlorophyll, as well as important fatty acids that may help in the fight against breast cancer. Many sea vegetables also have high concentrations of the minerals iron, potassium, calcium, magnesium and iodine.

SEEDS All seeds provide phyto-oestrogens – weak, nonsteroidal oestrogens that could help prevent both breast and prostate cancer by blocking and suppressing cancerous changes. Edible seeds like sesame, sunflower and pumpkin are also unrefined seed foods. So are fruits and vegetables that are eaten with their seeds, such as strawberries, blueberries, raspberries, kiwis, courgettes, tomatoes and cucumbers. Even seeds used for seasoning, such as cumin, coriander, caraway, anise and dill seed have phyto-oestrogens.

SOY products contain several phyto-oestrogens. There are some isoflavones in soy products, but research has shown that genistein is the most potent inhibitor of the growth and spread of cancerous cells. It appears to lower breast-cancer risk by inhibiting the growth of the epithelial cells and new blood vessels that tumours require to flourish.

SWEET POTATOES contain many anticancer properties, including beta-carotene, which may protect DNA in the cell nucleus from cancer-causing chemicals outside the nuclear membrane.

TEAS: Green tea contains certain antioxidants known as polyphenols (catechins) which appear to prevent cancer cells from dividing. Herbal teas do not show this benefit, but are very alkalising and have various other benefits. Even ordinary (black) tea contains antioxidants.

TOMATOES contain lycopene, an antioxidant which attacks roaming oxygen molecules, known as free radicals, that are suspected of triggering some cancers. It appears that the hotter the weather, the more lycopene tomatoes produce. They also have vitamin C, an antioxidant that can prevent cellular damage that leads to cancer. It is concentrated by cooking tomatoes. Scientists in Israel have shown that lycopene can kill mouth cancer cells. An increased intake of lycopene has already been linked to a reduced risk of breast, prostate, pancreas and colorectal cancer.

TURMERIC– a member of the ginger family, is believed to have medicinal properties because it inhibits production of the inflammation-related enzyme cyclo-oxygenase 2 (COX-2), levels of which are abnormally high in certain cancers, especially bowel and colon cancer.

WATERMELON – contains vitamins A, B6, C and thiamin. Studies have shown that a cup and a half of watermelon contains about 9 to 13 milligrams of lycopene. On average, watermelon has about 40 per cent more lycopene than raw tomatoes.

NB: The final part of this book is called 'Recipes for Living', a unique collection of ideas to bring light-filled foods into everyday family meals.

They are not Vegan, because some of them do include dairy products, eggs, and honey, none of which are eaten by Vegans.

However, they are all vegetarian because fresh fruits and vegetables are filled with light, and this is undoubtedly the simplest way to put light into our bodies!

RECIPES FOR LIVING
A Message from Bren

These recipes have been designed to help you to prepare foods, for yourself and your family, that bring life-giving light into the physical part of us – our body.

Although originally written for people dealing with cancer, this unique collection of recipes is perfect for anybody who wants to embrace a healthier lifestyle for themselves and for their families.

a note about allergies & intolerances

There is a difference between a food intolerance and a food allergy: allergies can be much more serious and foods that cause an allergic reaction should be avoided by anyone suffering from them. The symptoms of a food allergy almost always develop a few seconds or minutes after eating the food.

NB: None of the recipes mention possible allergens that they might include. So, if, for example, you see nuts, or dairy in a recipe, and you know it will cause an adverse reaction, you need to adapt it or prepare something completely different. Please also note that I accept no responsibility for ill effects of any allergens included in any of my recipes.

If you are preparing food for children, you can buy my little e-book *Fill That Gap*, which contains lots of ideas to avoid resorting to unhealthy snacks and processed ready meals. It is currently available from Amazon.

Common food allergies include:

Dairy, especially milk, Peanuts, Tree Nuts

Genuine food allergy symptoms include:

Tingling or itching in the mouth and eyes
Raised, itchy red rash (hives)
Swelling of the face, mouth, throat or eyes
Difficulty swallowing / gagging
Wheezing or shortness of breath
Feeling dizzy and lightheaded
Feeling sick (nausea) or vomiting
Sore tummy or urgent diarrhoea

Common food intolerances are caused by:

Dairy – Milk in particular
Gluten – Wheat in particular
Eggs
Oranges and Apricots
'Nightshade' Vegetables (Tomato, Capsicum etc)
Nuts
Legumes such as Lentils

Symptoms of food intolerance like eczema, tummy ache, diarrhoea, coughs, wheezing or runny nose, usually occur several hours after eating the food,

Readers should confirm with their usual health advisor that there are no physical reasons why they should not undertake a change of diet. If you suspect you have a disease or ailment of any kind, you should seek a professional opinion as soon as possible.

EVERY DAY BREAKFASTS

Smoothie Recipes to Whizz for One

Invest in an inexpensive blender because 'blitzing' fruit and vegetables is a great way to pack vitamins into your drinks.

Good morning sunshine!

4 ripe apricots, halved with stones out
1 small organic carrot, scrubbed
1 cup organic plain soya yoghurt or bio-yoghurt
1 cup plant milk
1 Tbsp organic maple syrup
1 dessert spoonful of lemon juice

Pineapple, Banana & Mango Smoothie

2 slices fresh pineapple
1 ripe peeled banana or 1 cup ripe strawberries
½ ripe mango, sliced
½ pint cold pressed apple juice

Summer Fruit Smoothie

2 ripe conference pears, peeled or use tinned pears in fruit juice not syrup
1 cup ripe strawberries
1 cup blackcurrants
½ pint cold pressed apple juice

Berry Good!

1½ cups chopped strawberries
1 cup blueberries
½ cup raspberries
2 Tbsp honey
1 tsp fresh lemon juice
Apple juice to thin it all down

Tastebud Tickler

Even someone whose taste buds are tainted by chemotherapy or other drugs will enjoy a tall glass of these next delicious and nutritious recipes! Just whizz and sip. As well as combatting post chemo nausea and fatigue, they are super-quick and tasty!

1 large ripe banana
3 or 4 chunks of ripe fresh pineapple
1 Tbsp coconut powder
Ice cold rice/ almond/ soya / coconut milk or a tin of coconut milk to make up a glass full

Tummy Soother

1 banana, sliced
1 serving plain yogurt
1 Tbsp honey
½ tsp freshly grated ginger or a sprig of fresh mint (or both)
Apple juice to make up a glass full.

Melon, Orange & Ginger Cooler

1 small sweet aromatic melon chopped into large chunks
1 thumb-sized piece ginger, peeled and finely chopped
Juice of 3 oranges (or a small glass of freshly squeezed)
2 Tbsp agave nectar or runny honey
1 squeeze / dash of lemon juice (optional)
Lots of ice, to serve

Blend the melon, ginger, orange juice and nectar / honey together until smooth – you may need to do this in batches.

Add the lemon juice if the orange is a bit sweet.

Serve in tall glasses over lots of ice.

Tropical Temptation in a Bowl

Although not a smoothie this is a chemo nausea-beater par excellence!
1 whole papaya fruit, peeled, de-seeded and sliced
   OR ½ a Gallia/ cantaloupe/ honeydew melon
   OR 1 whole mango, peeled and sliced
   OR 3 slices of freshly cut and cubed pineapple
Juice and zest of ½ a lime (un-waxed)
1 inch of fresh root ginger, finely grated

Place the fruit in a cereal bowl then add the lime juice & zest, plus the grated ginger – relax and relish!

You'll feel a whole lot better!

WEEKEND BREAKFASTS

Perfect Pancakes

Makes 6 - 8 crepe-style pancakes

3 Tbsp buckwheat or spelt flour
3 Tbsp rye flour
1 Tsp baking powder
1 Tsp each of sesame, poppy, flax and caraway seeds
2 Tbsp currants / sultanas / dried blueberries / cranberries / goji berries
2 free-range eggs
1 Tbsp olive or flax oil or organic butter
½ pint plant milk
Extra oil for frying

Mix dry ingredients in a bowl and make a well in the centre; break in the eggs and oil, stir and slowly add milk to reach a pouring consistency.

Melt a little oil/butter in a pan and ladle in batter to cover the bottom. Turn or toss when surface is covered in bubbles and not runny. Keep warm until all the pancakes are cooked. Serve with maple syrup or honey with lemon juice, or black cherry preserve & plain yoghurt.

Avocado on Toast

Cut an avocado in half round its middle and scoop out the flesh. Mash in a bowl with a little olive oil and lemon juice, then pile onto toasted rye bread.

Add a poached egg if you like – delicious and quick!

Morning Glory for Four

Prepare in the evening for next day's breakfast:

1 cup porridge oats
3 cups plant milk
(or a tin of blackcurrants, raspberries or strawberries, preserved in fruit juice and one cup of apple juice)
1 cup dried fruit such as: chopped apricots, dates, raisins, sultanas, blueberries or cranberries
3 Tbsp sunflower seeds and/or mixed nuts
2 Tbsp maple syrup
1 Tsp cinnamon

Combine all ingredients in a bowl. Cover and leave in the fridge overnight.
Serve with dairy-free milk / 'cream' or yoghurt and more fresh fruit

Power-Packed Porridge for Two

1 cup porridge oats
3 cups filtered water
½ cup dried fruit
1 Tbsp sunflower / pumpkin seeds or pine kernels

Put all ingredients into cooking pot and stir the mixture with wooden spoon or 'spurtle' (Scottish porridge stick) until it bubbles like the craters of the moon. Serve with ice-cold plant milk. Sprinkle with dark brown muscovado sugar if you like, or a slosh of maple syrup

SUPER SALADS

Red, White & Green Salad

1 head of raw cauliflower, broken into flowerets
4 cherry tomatoes, halved
1 small red onion, or 1 spring onion finely sliced
1 handful baby spinach leaves
1 large sprig parsley or coriander, chopped
1 tsp Dijon mustard or whole grain mustard
1 Tbsp plain live yoghurt
1 Tbsp lemon juice
1 Tbsp virgin olive oil

Put all the ingredients into a bowl and toss

Chicory, Apple & Avocado Salad

1 small head of chicory, sliced thinly
1 tangy eating apple, sliced
1 spring onion, chopped
1 avocado, flesh scooped out and chopped
1 handful fresh coriander, chopped
2 Tbsp organic maple syrup
1 Tbsp extra virgin olive oil
Juice of 1 small lime or 1 Tbsp of apple cider vinegar

Place all the ingredients in a salad bowl and toss

No-Mayo Coleslaw

¼ white cabbage, finely sliced
¼ red cabbage, finely sliced
2 medium carrots, grated
½ red onion, finely sliced
For the dressing
2 tbsp lemon juice
2 tsp good quality Dijon mustard
4 tbsp extra virgin olive oil

Place all the ingredients for the dressing in a bowl and whisk, or shake in a jar. Pour the dressing over the vegetables and mix together thoroughly.

Avocado, Celery, Apple, Date & Walnut Salad

1 avocado, stone removed, flesh scooped out and chopped
1 stick of celery, finely chopped
1 tangy eating apple, sliced
2 Tbsp chopped dates
2 Tbsp chopped walnuts * omit if allergic

Toss in a bowl with olive oil & lemon juice

Gingery Carrot Coleslaw

3 medium carrots, grated
2 cups red cabbage shredded finely
1 cup sultanas
2 Tbsp sunflower seeds
2 Tbsp pumpkin seeds

Toss in a bowl with lemon & ginger dressing (below)

Beetroot & Apple Salad

4 small, cooked beetroot – chopped
2 tangy eating apples chopped or sliced
1 carrot, grated
1 bunch fresh parsley chopped finely
1 Tbsp toasted sesame seeds

Toast the sesame seeds in a heavy pan on top of the stove until they go light brown, shaking constantly so as not to burn them. Mix all together and dress with your favourite salad dressing.

Beansprout, Beetroot & Apple Salad

1 mug homemade mung bean sprouts
1 medium beetroot, raw, coarsely grated
1 eating apple sliced thinly
2 Tbsp chopped nuts or sunflower seeds
Juice & zest of 1 un-waxed lemon
1 Tbsp organic runny honey
1 Tbsp olive oil

Place the sprouts, beetroot and apple in a bowl, sprinkle on the nuts or seeds. Mix the lemon juice with the honey and olive oil in a cup or small jar, pour over the salad and serve immediately

Oriental-Style Bean Sprouts with Cucumber

2 cups homemade mung bean sprouts
½ cucumber
1 Tbsp fresh lemon juice
1 Tbsp sesame oil
1 Tbsp Tamari soy sauce
1 Tbsp water
1' fresh root ginger, grated
1 Tbsp sesame seeds (toasted if you have time)
Place the bean sprouts in a bowl
Peel the cucumber (optional) and slice into matchsticks or dice finely. Mix with the sprouts.
In a small bowl or jar, mix lemon juice, sesame oil, soy sauce and water, beat or shake well and add to the sprouts and ginger. Garnish with the sesame seeds.

Alfalfa Sprouts with Egg & Olives

1 mug of home sprouted alfalfa
2 hard-boiled eggs, chopped
2 Tbsp pitted black olives, chopped
1 Tbsp plain organic yogurt
1 tsp whole grain mustard
Salt & pepper to taste
1 Tbsp flax oil or olive oil

Mix it all together and enjoy on oatcakes or rye bread.

Spicy Couscous Salad for Four

1 cup couscous (see how to cook below)
1 tsp mild curry powder
1 tsp organic veg bouillon or 1 crumbled veg stock cube
1 cup of boiling water
1 small red onion or 2 spring onions, chopped
1 tomato, chopped
1 yellow pepper, chopped
¼ cucumber, chopped
1 handful fresh coriander, chopped
1 dried, chopped apricot (optional)
1 Tbsp sultanas
1 Tbsp olive oil
1 Tbsp balsamic vinegar
1 Tbsp lemon juice

Put a cupful of dry couscous in a medium bowl or measuring jug with the curry powder and vegetable stock and add the boiling water. Stir and leave to soak while you prepare the rest. Then stir again and leave to cool.

Add the vegetables, coriander, and dried fruits to the cooled - down couscous and mix well. Add the olive oil, lemon juice and balsamic vinegar and put into the fridge to chill for an hour so the flavours can mingle.

Fruity Sprouty Salad

1 cup homemade alfalfa sprouts
1 crisp red apple, diced
1 ripe nectarine, cubed
1 small bunch black grapes, halved & seeded
2 small carrots, grated or cut into matchsticks

Place everything into a salad bowl and gently toss with a light oil - such as grapeseed - to preserve the Vitamin A, and a squeeze of lime or lemon juice.

Minty Sprout Salad

1 cup mixed small seed homemade sprouts
1 head chicory, finely sliced
½ small red onion, finely sliced
1 Tbsp chopped fresh garden mint
Juice & zest of 1 un-waxed lime
2 Tbsp olive oil

Toss with your favourite dressing

Courgette Feta & Mint Salad

2 courgettes
100g bag rocket leaves
200g pack feta cheese (or vegetarian alternative), crumbled
Bunch of mint leaves roughly shredded

Peel the courgettes into long ribbons with a potato peeler. Arrange with the rocket on a large platter.
Scatter over the feta and mint leaves, and drizzle on your favourite dressing.

SALAD DRESSINGS

Anti-Inflammatory Turmeric Dressing

1 tsp ground turmeric or 1" of grated fresh turmeric
½ tsp fine sea salt
¼ tsp ground black pepper
1 garlic clove crushed or 1 tsp dried dill
2 tsp honey
3 Tbsp cider vinegar
¼ cup extra virgin olive oil

Put all ingredients in to a glass jar with a tight-fitting lid. Shake well!! Pour over your favourite salad .

Bee Healthy Salad Dressing

2 tsp clear organic honey
2 cloves garlic, crushed
2 tsp wholegrain mustard
2 Tbsp Tamari soy sauce
2 Tbsp balsamic/cider vinegar or lemon juice
6 Tbsp extra-virgin olive oil

Mix up well and pour over mixed green salad

Lemon & Ginger Dressing

1 Tbsp honey or maple syrup
2 Tbsp lemon or lime juice
1 Tbsp grated ginger
4 Tbsp cold-pressed oil of your choice

Shake up in a tight-lidded jar or bottle

Salsa Verde

1 handful fresh parsley, chopped very finely
1 handful fresh mint, chopped very finely
4 cloves garlic, crushed
4 Tbsp pine nut kernels, crushed or chopped
1 spring onion, chopped finely
Zest and juice of ½ an un-waxed lemon or lime
¼ pint extra virgin olive oil

Combine all the ingredients and spoon over vegetables, polenta, pasta, roasted vegetables or salads!

Nutty Maple Magic Salad Dressing

1 tsp smooth peanut or almond butter
   or tahini if allergic to nuts
2 tsp organic maple syrup
1 Tbsp organic soy sauce
2 Tbsp extra-virgin olive oil or flax oil
1 Tbsp lemon juice

Put all ingredients into a small jar with tight-fitting lid and shake to blend!

Yogurt Dressing

1 small tub plain yogurt – dairy or plant based
2 Tbsp fresh lemon juice or 1 Tbsp organic cider vinegar
1 Tbsp extra virgin olive oil
½ tsp mustard powder
1 pinch sea salt
1 pinch freshly ground black pepper

Put everything into a bowl or lidded jar and mix or shake until well blended

Easy Tzatziki

Make the yogurt dressing above then add
Half a cucumber, de-seeded and finely chopped
A large sprig of finely chopped fresh mint leaves
Add 2 or 3 crushed cloves of garlic for extra zing!

Creamy Avocado Salad Dressing

1 Avocado – choose one that's ripe and creamy!
1 small tub plain unsweetened yogurt
1 Tbsp lemon juice
2 Tbsp extra virgin olive oil
3 cloves garlic, crushed
1 sprig of fresh coriander

This is easiest made in a small food processor or 'whizzer'. Blitz all the ingredients and gradually add enough water to thin it down to a creamy consistency Avocado is very dense! It actually needs quite a bit of thinning to make it pourable – about 6 tablespoons of water for half an avocado.

Easy Lemon Dressing

6 Tbsp extra virgin olive oil
1 pinch sea salt
1 pinch freshly ground black pepper
1 lemon, squeezed
1 Tbsp lemon zest
1 tsp mustard
1 garlic clove, crushed
1 tsp finely chopped parsley or coriander

Put everything into a bowl or lidded jar and mix or shake until well blended

TASTY SALSA TOPPINGS

A salsa is a tasty sauce or topping that can dramatically reduce your desire for salt. Try the following salsa ideas to add extra flavour to your meals.
Simply chop the ingredients finely and mix.

Mexican

Avocado, fresh tomato, red pepper and chilli

Italian

Fresh basil, fresh tomato, onion, pepper, balsamic vinegar and extra virgin olive oil.

Thai

Fresh coriander, sweet chilli sauce and crushed unsalted peanuts.

Chinese

Crushed garlic, onion, shallot, crushed ginger, sesame oil and a dash of salt-reduced soy sauce.

Indian

Cucumber, low fat natural yoghurt, mint, mango chutney and curry powder or paste.

Plant-based Parmesan Cheese Substitute

Ground Almonds
Nutritional Yeast
Fine sea salt to taste

Use equal parts of ground almonds and nutritional yeast. Mix well and add a little salt if you like.
You can use any nuts instead of almonds, grind them up in your coffee grinder!

Foraged Wild Garlic Pesto

150g wild garlic leaves gathered fresh and washed (several good handfuls)
50g grated parmesan cheese or vegetarian alternative
2 Tbsp lemon juice bottled or squeezed from ½ a lemon
50g ground almonds or walnuts
150ml olive oil
Mash together or blitz with sea salt and pepper to taste
Delicious served with roasted vegetables or your favourite pasta

Wild Garlic Flowers

Freshly gathered wild garlic flowers are delicious. They can be sprinkled over your salads like little white stars.

Nasturtium Leaves

Pick a handful of unblemished nasturtium leaves to add a peppery zesty flavour to your green salad!

COOL SUMMER SOUPS

Chunky Chilled Garden Gazpacho

1 standard tin chopped tomatoes
2 Tbsp olive oil
1 dash of red wine vinegar or balsamic vinegar (start small and taste!)
1 Tbsp runny honey
1 large fresh tomato, cut into small cubes
1 green pepper, chopped finely
1 sweet red pepper, chopped finely
1 stalk celery, chopped finely
1 clove garlic, crushed (or more if you like garlic)
1 cucumber, de-seeded & diced
1 spring onion, chopped
½ tsp Tabasco sauce or cayenne pepper
1 Tbsp lemon juice
½ pint vegetable stock, cooled

In a large mixing bowl or jug, combine tinned tomatoes, olive oil, vinegar and honey.

Stir in remaining ingredients and refrigerate until chilled.

Transfer to a serving dish, and garnish with finely chopped fresh chives, finely shredded lettuce, and chopped fresh coriander, basil or parsley.

Ladle into bowls and serve with crusty bread rolls.

Raw Chilled Minty Cucumber & Yogurt Soup

1 large ripe cucumber, peeled & cubed
1 spring onion, chopped finely
2 cloves garlic, crushed
1 pint vegetable stock (cooled)
I small tub plain yogurt dairy or plant-based
Flavour to taste (try lime or lemon juice, paprika or cayenne pepper)
1 small bunch fresh mint, finely chopped, leaving 4 sprigs to garnish

Mix all the ingredients together then put in a blender and whizz until smooth, adjust seasoning and chill. Ladle into bowls and garnish with the mint sprigs

Cool Green Pea Soup

2 tablespoon extra-virgin olive oil1 medium onion, finely chopped
1 clove garlic, minced
1 standard bag of frozen peas
1 handful mint leaves, roughly chopped
2 pints vegetable stock
Sea salt to taste
Freshly ground pepper to taste

Gently heat the oil, add the onion and cook for 10 minutes. Add the garlic and cook for another 3 minutes. Add frozen peas, mint, and stock. Cover and cook at a medium boil for 10 minutes.
Blend the soup in a food processor or blender, to create a thick puree. Chill and serve with sprigs of mint and swirl a spoonful of plain yogurt if you like.

COMFORTING WINTER SOUPS

Blissful Broth for Four

1 onion
1 leek
1 parsnip
2 carrots
1 small sweet-potato
1 stick celery
2 cloves garlic, crushed or chopped
2 tbsp olive oil, coconut oil or ghee
2 pints vegetable stock
1 Tbsp dried mixed herbs
3 Tbsp red lentils
2 Tbsp whole millet
1 Tbsp flax seeds
Rock or sea salt to taste

Peel or scrub all the vegetables and chop into medium chunks. Starting with the onions, stir fry all vegetables gently until soft. Add stock and garlic, dried herbs, lentils and millet.
Stir, bring to boil and cover. Reduce heat and simmer gently 1½ - 2 hours; season, check consistency and stir occasionally. If the broth looks too thick, or starts to stick to the pan, stir in a little more water.

Lovely Lentil Soup

1 large onion, finely chopped
3 cloves of garlic chopped or crushed
1 large carrot, sliced
1 large potato (baking size)
1 Tbsp light olive oil
1 cup of lentils, red, brown, or green
1 pint vegetable stock
Fresh or dried herbs – parsley, oregano, bay leaf
Salt and pepper to taste

Sauté the prepared vegetables in a large pan for a few minutes then add the lentils with the stock and stir well. Add the seasoning and herbs. Put a lid on the pan, turn down the heat and simmer for about half an hour or longer, until the lentils are mushy, and the vegetables are well cooked. Serve with crusty bread or buttered oatcakes.

Quick and Easy Vegetable Soup for Two

1 onion finely chopped
1 carrot, grated
1 parsnip grated
1 stick of celery very finely sliced or chopped
1 pint of vegetable stock
Mixed herbs, sea salt and black pepper

Put the vegetables in a pot and stir fry quickly until tender; add the stock, herbs, sea salt and black pepper to taste. Bring to the boil and simmer for half an hour.

Golden Winter Warmer Soup for Four

1 onion, sliced
1 stick celery, chopped
1 parsnip, chopped
2 carrots, sliced
1 small butternut squash, de-seeded and chopped
2 Tbsp olive/ sunflower oil
2 pints vegetable stock
5 Tbsp whole dried millet grains or quinoa
1 Tbsp dried parsley or handful fresh parsley, chopped

Heat oil in large pan, then starting with the onions stir-fry all the vegetables until the onions are soft. Add stock and millet; stir, bring to the boil and cover tightly; reduce heat and simmer gently for an hour or so, stirring & checking consistency occasionally. Add parsley just before serving. This is a chunky, substantial soup.

Easy Peasy Green Soup for Four

1 leek chopped fine
1 Tbsp olive oil, or ghee or coconut oil
4 cloves garlic, crushed or chopped
1 small head spring greens cut into fine ribbons
1 mug frozen green peas
1 Tbsp dried mixed herbs
1 Tbsp dried mint
1 tsp organic soy sauce
2 pints vegetable stock
Ground black pepper and sea salt to taste (optional)

Heat oil in large pan and stir-fry onions gently until soft, add leek and cook a minute or two longer, until heated through, but not burnt. Add all other ingredients and bring to the boil. Reduce heat, cover and simmer, until cooked - liquidise if you like it smooth.

Mighty Minestrone

1 Tbsp cooking oil
1 large onion, peeled and chopped
1 red pepper, de-seeded and chopped
1 courgette, sliced
1 large carrot, chopped
1 Tbsp tomato paste
5 cloves garlic, crushed or chopped
1 handful gluten-free pasta spirals or shells
1 standard tin organic baked beans
1 standard tin plum tomatoes
1 ½ pints vegetable stock
1 Tbsp Italian seasoning/dried mixed herbs
1 Tbsp organic soy sauce

Stir-fry all the vegetables until cooked but not burnt; add the tinned tomatoes, baked beans and pasta, plus the stock followed by the herbs and seasonings.

Bring to the boil, stirring once or twice, then lower heat, cover and simmer for 1 hour or until cooked.

Serve with piles of crusty wholemeal or sourdough bread.

Easy Creamy Mushroom Soup

2oz butter
2 leeks, chopped
3 garlic cloves, crushed
1 pack chestnut mushrooms, sliced
2-3 sprigs fresh thyme leaves
1 pint vegetable stock

Melt the butter in a large pot and gently cook the leeks and garlic for 4-5 minutes or until softened but not browned. Add the mushrooms and thyme and cook on high for 3-5 minutes until the mushrooms are softened and have released much of their water.

Pour over the stock and cook for 5 minutes. Then remove from the heat, carefully pour into a food processor and blend until smooth. Alternatively, keep in the pot and use a stick blender to blitz until smooth.

Divide between four bowls and serve.

LIGHT MEALS

For four people unless otherwise mentioned

Quick Flax Fried Rice

2 cups cooked organic long grain brown rice
2 Tbsp organic sunflower oil, rapeseed oil or ghee
3 eggs, beaten well
8 oz frozen mixed vegetables (diced carrots, peas, corn etc), thawed
2 spring onions, chopped
2 Tbsp soy sauce
½ Tsp sesame oil
2 Tbsp flax seeds (linseeds)
2 beaten eggs if you like them

In a large frying pan, or wok, over low heat, heat the oil gently. Add the eggs and stir until just starting to cook then add the vegetables and spring onions, followed quickly by the cooked rice, stirring to coat the rice as the eggs set.

Add soy sauce, sesame oil and flax seeds, cover and cook over a low heat, turning over gently but frequently, until everything is steaming but not burnt.

Season and stir in the two eggs, beaten with a little water if you are using them.

Serve with delicious lightly steamed green vegetables such as baby spinach, Swiss chard or broccoli – even kale goes well with this wholesome dish.

Easy Mushroom & Spinach Savoury Rice

2 cups cooked organic short grain brown rice
2 Tbsp grapeseed, coconut oil or ghee for stir-frying
1 large onion, chopped
6 or 8 sliced mushrooms (oyster or shiitake are good)
4 handfuls of fresh baby spinach, chopped
1 standard tin chickpeas, drained or 1 cup frozen peas
1 tsp powdered turmeric
Ground black pepper and sea salt / soy sauce to taste

Stir-fry onions until tender then add the mushrooms and continue to sauté the mixture until tender, then add the spinach and chickpeas / green peas and stir until the spinach is wilted. Stir in the cooked rice and continue to stir it all around until thoroughly heated through, add the turmeric, season, and mix well before serving.

Quick Spinach with Sesame Seeds

1 bag of baby spinach leaves
2 Tbsp sunflower or light olive oil or coconut oil
2 Tbsp soy sauce
1 Tbsp lemon juice
1 clove garlic, crushed
1 Tbsp sesame seeds, lightly toasted in a dry pan

Rinse spinach, drain thoroughly and pat dry (if not already washed). In small bowl, combine soy sauce, lemon juice, and garlic. Heat oil in wok or skillet over a gentle heat. Add spinach and stir to gently keep spinach moving for about 1 minute, or until tender, but still green. Remove from heat and sprinkle with soy mixture and toasted sesame seeds, season to taste with ground pepper and sea salt. Mix well. Serve with your favourite rice or noodles.

Mushroom Quinoa

1 Tbsp organic rapeseed oil
12 medium mushrooms, sliced
2 spring onions, chopped
2 cups vegetable stock
1 cup quinoa (rinsed first)
1 head of broccoli, broken into tiny sprigs

Heat oil gently in a large pan. Add the sliced mushrooms and chopped onions. Stir fry until soft. Add stock and bring to the boil. Stir in quinoa. Reduce the heat, cover, and simmer until the quinoa is tender, about 15 minutes. Add the broccoli and stir-fry everything lightly until broccoli is tender but not mushy.

Frittata with Mushrooms & Peppers

2 spring onions or 1 shallot
6 mushrooms, sliced (shiitake or oyster are great)
3 cloves garlic, crushed
1 red pepper, chopped, or a medium courgette, sliced
Bunch parsley, chopped
Oil or ghee (clarified butter) for frying
4 eggs - beaten with 4 Tbsp water

Chop the spring onions / shallot and stir fry in a heavy frying pan until starting to soften. Add the mushrooms, pepper, garlic & parsley, then cover and leave to cook on a gentle heat while you beat the eggs with the water until smooth

Pour the egg mixture onto the vegetables and turn up the heat, stirring around constantly until the egg is completely cooked. Serve with salad and rye bread.

Quinoa with Peas & Sweetcorn

1 cup dry quinoa
2 cups vegetable stock
2 Tbsp butter or vegetable/ vegan spread
½ cup frozen sweet corn kernels
½ cup frozen peas
4 garlic cloves crushed
2 whole spring onions sliced

Place the quinoa and stock in a pan. Bring to the boil. Lower the heat and simmer, covered, until the liquid is absorbed. Leave to the side.

Melt the butter/ spread in a frying pan and add the frozen peas and corn (no need to defrost). Over medium heat, sauté for about 5 minutes until cooked.

Push the corn and peas to the side and add the minced garlic. Sauté until fragrant (about a minute). Combine the garlic, peas, and corn in the skillet. Add the chopped spring onions, cook for two minutes. Remove from the heat.

Spoon the cooked quinoa into the peas and corn mixture. Combine ingredients in the pan. Season with salt or a dash of soy sauce if you like and add an extra knob of butter/ spread.

MAIN MEALS & SIDE DISHES

All these recipes serve four unless stated otherwise

Buckwheat or Spelt Pasta, Tomato & Mushroom Sauce

8 oz buckwheat or spelt pasta (dry weight)
2 tablespoons olive oil
1 large onion, chopped
2 cloves garlic
8 plum tomatoes, cut into wedges (or 1 standard tin)
8 chestnut or Shitake mushrooms, sliced or chopped
Several sprigs of chopped fresh basil
or a tsp of dried oregano
Sea salt and black pepper or cayenne pepper to taste

Cook the pasta and heat the olive oil in a frying pan over medium heat, stir-fry the onion for about 5 minutes, until translucent.

Add the garlic, tomato wedges / tinned tomato, and mushrooms, cover, and simmer gently until the tomatoes and mushrooms are cooked through.

Sprinkle on the basil/ oregano, salt and pepper and stir through the pasta

Fast Courgette and Leek Pasta

1 courgette, sliced very finely or shredded
½ Leek very finely sliced (white end, keep the green end for soup)
Fresh herbs – chop up a handful of whatever you like
Olive oil

Place a colander in the sink and put prepared courgette and leek into it. Boil the pasta until cooked and drain over the vegetables in the colander. Return to everything the pan and toss with olive oil and fresh herbs, season to taste. Chilli flakes are great if you like them!

Savoury Rice Bake

1 bag of fresh baby spinach leaves
1 cup cooked short grain brown rice
1 cup feta cheese, crumbled
4 free-range organic eggs, lightly beaten with a splash of water
2 Tbsp olive oil
1 sprig rosemary, chopped
½ cup plant milk (unsweetened)
1 onion chopped, or 2 spring onions, chopped
1 clove garlic, crushed
1 tsp light soy sauce

Sauté the onion and garlic, add the spinach, stir-fry lightly until wilted, then mix in the cooked rice, cheese, eggs, oil, rosemary, milk, and soy sauce.

Put the mixture into a lightly oiled casserole dish and bake in a hot oven until golden. Goes well with roasted butternut squash (below) – cook at the same time

Roasted Butternut Squash with Ginger

1 large butternut squash
1 inch ginger root, grated
¼ cup cloudy pressed apple juice
½ tsp ground nutmeg

Peel and seed the squash. Cut into small cubes. Mix with the ginger and apple juice and place in a lightly oiled casserole dish.

Cover and bake in a hot oven for about an hour. Sprinkle on the nutmeg just before serving.

Great served with the savoury rice bake. (Above)

Garlic Ginger Tofu

1 Tbsp rapeseed oil or light olive oil
2 cloves garlic, minced
1 inch root ginger, grated or chopped fine
Juice of half a lime
1 Tbsp soy sauce, or to taste
1 pack (450g / 1 lb) firm tofu

Heat oil in a wok or frying pan over medium heat. Stir in garlic and ginger and cook for 1 minute.

Add tofu to the pan with soy sauce and stir to coat. Cover, and continue cooking for 20 to 30 minutes. Squeeze lime juice over before serving with rice or noodles.

Shiitake Mushrooms with Tofu

2 portions cooked brown rice cooked as above
1 packet firm tofu, cut into 1-inch cubes
4 cloves garlic, crushed
1 inch root ginger grated
1 Tbsp lemon juice
1 Tbsp Tamari soy sauce
1 Tbsp sesame seeds
2 Tbsp olive oil
2 small onions or shallots, finely chopped
2 stalks celery, finely chopped
6 or 8 fresh Shiitake mushrooms
1 large handful curly kale leaves, chopped
2 Tbsp coconut or sesame oil for stir frying

While the rice is cooking, mix and marinate the tofu cubes in a bowl with the lemon juice, ginger, garlic, soy sauce, sesame seeds & 1 Tbsp olive oil.

Meanwhile stir-fry the onions in the rest of the oil until golden; add the mushrooms and celery and stir fry for a few more minutes, then add the kale.

Cover and cook for a few more minutes, until the kale is wilted, stir in the tofu mixture, including the marinade and cook for 5-10 minutes more, stirring frequently, until heated through and the marinade liquid almost evaporated. Gently fold in the rice and heat through to combine flavours before serving.

Garlic Mushrooms

150 g Shitake mushrooms quartered or use button mushrooms
1 Tbsp unsalted butter or olive oil
3 or 4 cloves garlic
1 Tbsp fresh herbs: parsley, thyme, oregano, rosemary, basil, coriander – whatever you like

Toss the prepared mushrooms in the oil until half cooked and add the garlic and sauté a few more minutes. Season to taste and sprinkle with fresh herbs.

Oaty Stuffed Mushrooms

4 Portobello (large flat) Mushrooms
1 medium onion, chopped fine
6 cherry tomatoes finely chopped
3 garlic cloves, minced
½ cup rolled oats
½ cup chopped walnuts
Fresh thyme – a few sprigs stripped, with stalks discarded, or a tsp of Italian seasoning
Sea or rock salt and freshly ground pepper
Olive oil

Cut off the mushroom stalks, chop finely and mix with the other ingredients and just enough oil to bind it all together. Divide the mixture between the mushrooms, pressing down with the spoon, and arrange on an oiled or lined baking tray. Cook in a hot oven until sizzling, about ½ an hour. Serve with salad for lunch or plain boiled rice for a main meal.

Noodles With Ginger, Garlic & Broccoli

8 oz rice or soba noodles
3 cloves garlic, crushed
2 or 3 broccoli heads, divided into small sprigs
4 Tbsp pine kernels
4 Tbsp olive or coconut oil
4 Tbsp sesame oil
1 inch fresh root ginger, grated
1 bunch chopped fresh or 2 Tbsp dried dill
I small green chilli pepper chopped (optional)
Tamari soy sauce

Cook the noodles according to directions on the packet.

Drain, return to pan, coat with some of the sesame oil & set aside.

Heat the olive / coconut oil in a wok. Sauté the garlic and stir in the pine kernels, ginger, chilli and dill, then add the broccoli sprigs and stir fry, adding a little water to stop them burning.

Add the cooked noodles, drizzle with the remaining sesame oil and the soy sauce and toss until well combined and heated through.

Tasty Spicy Baked Cauliflower Steaks

1 whole cauliflower
Salt and cayenne pepper to taste
2 Tbsp oil/coconut oil
1 teaspoon freshly grated root ginger
1 teaspoon ground cumin
½ teaspoon ground turmeric
Small bunch of coriander, chopped

Remove the leaves and trim the stem end of the cauliflower, leaving the core intact. Using a large knife, cut the cauliflower into four one-inch-thick 'steaks'. Season each steak with salt and cayenne on both sides.

Heat 1 tablespoon of olive oil or coconut oil in a large frying pan over medium-high heat. Sear the cauliflower steaks until golden brown, about 2 minutes on each side. Gently transfer the steaks onto a baking sheet.

Mix the other 1 tablespoon of oil with the ginger, cumin, and turmeric. Brush or spoon the mixture onto the cauliflower steaks until they are well coated.

Roast in a medium hot oven until tender, about 15 minutes and sprinkle with chopped parsley or coriander.

Serve with brown rice and a tasty relish like wild garlic pesto or salsa verde for a satisfying main course.

Roasted Vegetable Biryani

1 large red onion cut into wedges
1 courgette, cut into chunks
1 carrot, chopped coarsely
1 aubergine, thickly sliced
2 sticks celery, chunked
2 Tbsp coconut oil or ghee
2 Tbsp mild curry paste, or 2 tsp curry powder
1 tsp turmeric
4 oz basmati rice, uncooked
½ - ¾ pint hot vegetable stock
2 Tbsp chopped fresh coriander
1 Tbsp desiccated coconut

Preheat oven to 190° C. Toss vegetables in the oil and spread out in a large ovenproof dish, cook for 20 minutes or until starting to turn golden.

Remove from oven, stir in the rice, curry paste/powder and turmeric then pour on the stock and return to oven for ½ hour, or until rice is cooked and stock has been absorbed. Add chopped coriander and coconut and serve with chapattis or wholemeal pitta breads.

SAVOURY SNACKS & TREATS!

'Midshipman's Butter'

In the 1700's English seamen discovered that the avocado could be used as a spread to soften the hard biscuit they had for meals. It was a big improvement on rancid butter.

Today crushed avocado makes a great instant spread for oatcakes, crackers & toasted sourdough, or rye bread. Simply cut the fruit in half and use the creamy green flesh instead of butter.

Guacamole

1 large ripe avocado
1 clove garlic - crushed (more if you love garlic)
2 Tbsp olive oil
1 Tbsp lemon or lime juice
1 Small bunch fresh coriander

Cut the avocado in half, remove the stone, and scoop out the flesh into a small mixing bowl. Add the garlic, pour in the olive oil and lemon / lime juice. Mash everything with a fork until all big chunks of avocado have gone and, finally, add the coriander, chopped up.

This is a wonderful dip with 'crudities' – sticks of healthy raw carrot and celery, or flowerets of raw broccoli and cauliflower. It is also delicious spread on toasted sourdough bread, or baked potatoes.

Butter Bean Humous

Chickpeas, cannelloni or borlotti beans are just as good

1 tin butter beans, drained
2 large cloves garlic, crushed
2 Tbsp sesame butter (Tahini)
1 Tbsp lemon juice
1 Tbsp olive oil
1 tsp toasted sesame oil
Optional extras:
1 small chunk fresh root ginger, grated
½ tsp ground cumin
1 tsp tamari soy sauce
½ tsp cayenne pepper or smoked paprika

Mash or whizz all the ingredients until a coarse paste is achieved.

Pack into a bowl and serve with rye or lentil crackers and a bowl of green salad, or 'crudities' – sticks of healthy carrot and celery

Fresh Green Pea Humous

1 cup frozen peas, thawed or better still, freshly shelled
4 Tbsp crushed pine kernels
2 Tbsp fresh lemon juice
4 garlic cloves, crushed
Sprig of fresh mint
½ tsp salt
½ tsp cayenne pepper or smoked paprika

Mash or pound the ingredients until smooth if you don't own a 'whizzer'.

Serve with oatcakes, crackers or carrot and celery sticks

Aubergine Crisps

These aubergine crisps are healthy and delicious! And super easy to make!
Just thinly slice an aubergine and cook the slices for a few minutes on each side in a lightly oiled frying pan until golden. Dry on a piece of kitchen towel before you lay them on some rocket, sprinkle them with pomegranate seeds and drizzle with fat free yogurt.

Baked Kale Crisps

1 handful kale leaves
1 Tbsp olive oil
1 Tbsp sesame seeds
Sea salt or Tamari soy sauce

Preheat oven to medium hot

Rinse and dry the kale, then remove the thicker stems and tough centre ribs. Cut or tear into large pieces.

Toss with the olive oil and sesame seeds in a bowl then sprinkle lightly with salt or Tamari.

Arrange in a single layer on a large baking sheet and bake for 20 minutes, or until crisp.

Cool down before eating. Store in an air-tight container.

Sprouty Soft Cheese Sandwich Filling

Spread two slices of rye bread with soft goats' cheese or organic cottage cheese and pile a generous amount of alfalfa sprouts on top. Sprinkle with a little soy sauce, make into a sandwich & enjoy!

Spicy Roasted Vegetable Crisps

Slice raw parsnip, carrot, beetroot and sweet potatoes very thinly using a sharp knife, vegetable peeler or with a mandolin. Toss in a bowl with olive oil, chilli powder or paprika, and sea salt

Arrange in a single layer on baking parchment or greaseproof paper on a baking tray.

Roast in a medium / hot oven for 20 minutes, turning over, after 10 minutes. They may not need the full time depending how thin they are - they are ready when the parsnips and sweet potato are golden brown. Cool to let them crisp.

Rosemary Walnuts

2 cups walnut halves
2 tsp dried rosemary, crushed
½ tsp fine sea or rock salt
¼ to ½ tsp cayenne pepper
Light olive oil for brushing

Place walnuts in a small bowl. Brush lightly with olive oil then add the seasonings. Toss to coat. Place in a single layer on a baking sheet.

Bake in a hot oven for 10 minutes. Serve warm, or cool completely and store in an airtight container.

Spicy Roasted Chickpeas

1 standard tin chickpeas, drained
1 Tbsp light olive oil
¼ tsp ground sea or rock salt
¼ tsp chili powder or smoked paprika
¼ tsp ground cumin
¼ tsp ground coriander
¼ tsp garlic powder

Drain chickpeas in a colander and let them dry, patting with a paper towel. Toss in a bowl with the olive oil and other ingredients. Arrange on a baking sheet in a single layer and roast in a hot oven for about 35 to 45 minutes, shaking the tray every ten minutes, to make sure they don't burn. They will be golden brown and crunchy on the inside when done, not moist.

Roasted Cumin Cashews

2 cups whole cashews
2 Tbsp cup brown sugar
3 teaspoons chilli powder
1 tsp fine rock or sea salt
2 tsp ground cumin
1/2 tsp cayenne pepper
Olive oil for brushing

Put the nuts in a bowl and brush with the oil. Add the other ingredients and toss well to coat. Spread out on a greased baking tray. Bake in a hot oven for 50-55 minutes, shaking once. Tip out onto a baking sheet and cool. They will be crispy when cold.

SWEET TREATS

Sugar & Wheat-Free Blueberry Muffins

8 oz rice flour
2 tsp baking powder
2 Tbsp desiccated coconut
4 Tbsp sunflower or coconut oil
1 sweet apple stewed and mashed
    or 1 mashed ripe banana
2 large eggs, beaten
5 Tbsp plant milk
½ tsp vanilla extract
1 small punnet blueberries

Grease a muffin tray, or line with paper cases – this makes 12 little cakes.

Put the flour in a bowl with the coconut and baking powder then gradually stir in the wet ingredients (but not the blueberries) and beat until smooth. Finally, fold in the berries and spoon evenly into the cases.

Bake in a hot oven for about 25 minutes or until risen and cooked (test with a skewer or pointy knife, if it comes out clean, they are ready). Cool and enjoy

Easy Spelt Banana Muffins

1½ cups spelt flour
1 tsp baking powder
½ tsp baking soda
3 large very ripe bananas, mashed
½ cup soft brown sugar
1 egg
3 oz butter, melted or 3 Tbsp olive / sunflower oil

Preheat oven to hot
Grease a muffin tray or use 12 paper cupcake cases.
Mix together the dry ingredients and set aside.
In a large mixing bowl, combine bananas, sugar, egg and melted butter/oil.
Add flour mixture and beat until smooth.
Spoon into tray/ cake cases.
Bake in preheated oven for about 20 minutes.
They will spring back when lightly tapped
This mixture can also make one banana loaf. Alter cooking time accordingly.

Date & Sesame Spread for a Teatime Treat

Mix equal quantities of Tahini (sesame butter) and date syrup, or dates mashed up until smooth with a little boiling water, and cooled if you can't find date syrup.

This makes a perfect substitute for chocolate spread on oatcakes, rice cakes or warm buttered toast!

Blueberry Baked Apples

4 large dessert apples
4 Tbsp fresh blueberries
4 tsp soft brown sugar
4 Tbsp apple or lemon juice
Runny honey
Cinnamon if liked

Core the apples from the stalk end, leaving the bottom intact if you can and making a wider opening at the top. Place on foil on a baking tray

Cram as many blueberries into each apple as possible. Sprinkle a teaspoonful of sugar over the top of them and cinnamon if using. Pour the juice over to dissolve the sugar, bake in a moderate oven for 45 minutes and serve warm with dollops of plain yogurt and finally drizzle with runny honey - sweetly satisfying!

Variation: use dates or sultanas or dried apricots

Oaty Banana Biscuits

3 very ripe bananas
8 oz rolled oats
4 oz chopped dates
3 Tbsp coconut oil
1 teaspoon vanilla extract
Sesame seeds to sprinkle before cooking

Preheat oven to moderate
In a large bowl, mash the bananas and stir in oats, dates, oil, and vanilla, mix well, and allow to sit for 15 minutes. Drop spoonsful onto a baking tray and sprinkle with sesame seeds. Bake for 20 minutes, or until lightly brown. Makes two or three dozen biscuits, depending on size.

Fabulous Flapjacks

8 oz porridge oats
4 Tbsp runny honey / maple syrup
4 oz demerara sugar
2 oz unsalted butter

Melt the butter, syrup/ honey and sugar in a saucepan; turn off the heat and stir in the oats. Mix together and empty into a greased traybake tin pressing down with the back of a spoon so that it's about half an inch thick.

Bake in a pre-heated moderate oven for 15 - 20 minutes; slice with a knife or spatula while still hot and leave to cool before removing to an airtight container – or eating!

Heather's One Bowl Spiced Apple Cake

2 eggs,
1 ¾ cups soft brown sugar,
2 tsp cinnamon
1 tsp ground ginger
½ cup oil
6 medium apples
2 cups spelt flour
2 ½ tsp baking powder

Preheat oven to 350°.

In a large bowl, mix the eggs, sugar, cinnamon and oil. Peel and slice the apples and add to mixture in bowl. Add the baking powder and flour to the ingredients in the bowl, mixing thoroughly.
Pour into a greased 1lb loaf tin.

Bake for about 55 minutes or until risen and golden.

Easy 3-Ingredient Oatcakes

Makes 25 -50, depending on the size of your cutter

200 g oat flour OR grind your own rolled oats
100 g wholemeal or spelt flour
50 ml olive oil
Pinch of salt optional but adds flavour

Preheat the oven to 180C/350F/gas 4.

Blitz the oats in a food processor or coffee grinder if you don't have oat flour and tip into a baking bowl. Mix in the rest of the ingredients by hand and drizzle in 150ml-175ml water a bit at a time, stopping when the mixture just starts to come together as a dough.

Roll out* the dough (it might be a bit crumbly but should just about hold together. Cut into circles using a cookie cutter or upside-down glass tumbler.

*Rolling it between two sheets of greaseproof paper is the best way to keep it intact.

Bake for 20-35 mins, until firm, golden and cooked. Cool completely to crisp up.

Peanut Butter & Maple Syrup Spread

Mix organic smooth whole peanut butter with half as much organic maple syrup for a delicious spread for oatcakes, rice crackers or rye bread.

further reading

Cellular Awakening by Barbara Wren

Rabbits Don't Get Lymphoma by Cathie Grout

The Secret Life of Your Cells by Robert Stone PhD

Anything Can Be Healed by Martin Brofman

Mind Waves by Betty Shine

You Can Heal Your Life by Louise L. Hay

New Light on Angels by Diana Cooper

The Celestine Prophecy by James Redfield

Feng Shui Modern by Cliff Tan (Author), Dura Lee

Emotional Freedom by Garry A. Flint and Gary Craig

FINAL WORDS FROM BREN

remember to turn on your light!

Thank you for reading my book – I do hope you enjoyed it. I know for sure that my journey back to good health has been worth it, and I am so privileged to be able to share my story with anyone who needs help and encouragement on their own voyage through life.

I realise that my learning will never be over. I must always choose light rather than darkness, think positively instead of negatively and, most importantly of all I have to be mindful of my attitude to every situation and experience in case I slip back into my old, unhelpful ways of thinking, behaving and feeling.

It is my heartfelt hope that this simple programme for light and life will help anyone and everyone to recover, retain or create perfect health of mind, body, and spirit, and to shine again, should they so need.

Bren xx

Printed in Great Britain
by Amazon